AN
INVITATION
TO THE
SPIRIT-FILLED
LIFE

THE PROMISE

THE POWER

THE GIFTS

THE FRUIT

CHARLES WHITEHEAD

Published in 2016 by The Word Among Us Press
7115 Guilford Drive
Frederick, Maryland 21704
ww.wau.org

ISBN: 978-1-59325-289-2
eISBN: 978-1-59325-480-3

Cover design by Coronation Media

Made and printed in the United States of America.

Library of Congress Control Number: 2016933968

To Sue, with gratitude and love—
my wife, greatest supporter,
faithful companion on life's exciting journey,
and my best friend.

Contents

Foreword

Charles Whitehead has been one of the most influential Catholic laymen of the era since the Second Vatican Council. For eleven years, he was president of the International Council for the Catholic Charismatic Renewal. In that capacity, he worked closely with the Pontifical Council for the Laity and met frequently with Pope John Paul II. One of the outstanding features of the papacy of St. John Paul II was the growth of new movements and communities in the Church, which he saw as a fruit of the Vatican Council. Although the Charismatic Renewal is not a movement as such, many new communities have been inspired by it and are part of it. It was significant that at a gathering of new movements and communities in Rome on the eve of Pentecost 1998, Charles Whitehead was invited to respond to the pope's address on behalf of them all.

It is with that background and in light of that experience that Charles Whitehead has written *An Invitation to the Spirit-Filled Life*. It will soon become clear to the reader, however, that this book also finds roots in the whole Pentecostal revival of the twentieth century. This is a book, therefore, that is genuinely ecumenical. Moreover, it is clear throughout that its deepest roots are in Scripture and especially in the teaching of St. Paul on the gifts of the Holy Spirit.

This book is not intended to be a comprehensive and finely balanced exposition of the theology of the Holy Spirit. Rather, it is a plea for Christians to expect and pray for the gifts of the Holy Spirit. Charles Whitehead reminds us that more than 120 million Catholics have come to deeper faith through the Renewal and that in Christianity generally, this is overwhelmingly the fastest area of growth. That is why this book is timely. In it the author explains clearly what is meant by the baptism in the Holy Spirit and explores all the issues relating to the gifts of the Holy Spirit. He writes with passion, conviction, and authority. Most important, Charles Whitehead is not proposing any great new program or agenda for the Church or for Christians generally. His book is simply an encouragement to be open to the gifts that God has given us in Jesus Christ.

+Most Rev. Kevin McDonald
Archbishop Emeritus of Southwark, London

Introduction

Many people are questioning whether the new emphasis on the importance of the Holy Spirit is just another religious fad that will fade away like many before it. They wonder whether the Spirit really has an important part to play in the way they live their lives as Christians today. And why, they ask, if this focus on the person and work of the Spirit is so essential, haven't they heard about it before? These are good questions. I hope that these pages will help to answer them.

What follows was first written in 1979, but it is only now that I have decided to update, edit, and publish it. My original reasons for writing it were straightforward: even though I had received one of the best Catholic educations available, I had drifted away from the Church during my university years and only found my way back in 1976. By that time I was thirty-four years old, happily married to my wife, Sue, and the father of our first two children. I had a promising career in the papermaking and marketing industry. But I knew something was missing.

Why had I drifted from the Church? After all, the Jesuits had done a good job teaching me theology, doctrine, and apologetics. Yet I found these of little help in my day-to-day life. The answer, I discovered, was simple. I had completely failed to grasp the basic fact that the Holy Spirit, present in me through my baptism and confirmation, would bring me the power I needed to live an active and effective Christian life—but he needed my cooperation. Without it, the effects of the grace received were bound to be limited. Until

I understood this and allowed the Spirit the freedom to work in and through me, it was always going to be an uphill battle—one that I had very little chance of winning. I needed to begin by really knowing that God my Father loved me personally with an unconditional, freely given love.

It was as if I were pushing my car along the road because no one had told me there was fuel in the tank. All I needed to do was to turn the ignition key and start the engine! We are not supposed to live the Christian life without the power of the Holy Spirit. Why else would Jesus tell his disciples to wait in Jerusalem until they received "power from on high" (Luke 24:49) and from there take his message of love, new life, and salvation throughout the world? On the day of Pentecost, we read that the disciples were all "filled with the Holy Spirit" (Acts 2:4), and they immediately set out to do exactly what Jesus had said they were to do. They realized that the Spirit had come to empower them and that, if they cooperated with him, then anything and everything was possible. An infilling with the Holy Spirit should always be followed by an outflowing, a reaching out to others with the gospel message in word and deed.

It was this same simple fact that Sue and I discovered in 1976 through the remarkable witness of a small group of Christians from different local churches—Anglican, Baptist, and Catholic. How had I missed this central truth of the Christian faith? Why had no one pointed it out to me before? As a baptized and confirmed Catholic, the issue was not did I have the Holy Spirit—of course I had. The real question was, did the Holy Spirit have me? And the answer to that was quite clear: no, he had not. Once I realized this and deliberately surrendered my life to Jesus and his Holy Spirit, it was as if someone had turned on my spiritual engine. I took off, and life would never be quite the same again! I had given the power, which I had usurped, back to God. I had learned that "the God of Israel gives power and strength to his people" (Psalm 68:35), and that this power and strength come through the Holy Spirit.

We all start our spiritual journeys not really knowing who we are, what we have, what is available to us, or exactly where we're going. It's the Holy Spirit who reveals all of this, if we but ask him. From that moment of revelation, it has been a wonderful, exciting, challenging, and fulfilling journey for my wife and me. For that I am so grateful to God, as well as to that small ecumenical group who showed us a living faith and to the many remarkable people we have met along the way. Although we had no idea what the years ahead had in store for us, Sue and I realized in 1976 that a great adventure was beginning, and we wanted to give others the key that would start their spiritual engines too. So *An Invitation to the Spirit-Filled Life* was born in 1979, and as I look around me now, I realize that the need to understand the person and work of the Holy Spirit in our lives is even greater today than it was then. Things haven't changed for the better. We live in a precarious world, and if ever there was a need for Christians living in the fullness of the power of the Holy Spirit, it is in our nations today. We need spiritual renewal.

One of the challenges I've faced in writing this short book is how to maintain a correct balance between theology and experience. God created us with emotions as well as minds. Unfortunately, our demands to understand everything, even the deepest mysteries of God, and to be able to explain it all in a rationally enlightened way, can mean that we miss out on God's supernatural activity. We often suppress the emotional and experiential side of our nature because we don't want to appear naïve and foolish. Of course, we must be adult about our faith, but Jesus expects us to be childlike in our approach to the divine mysteries, often accepting things that we do not fully understand: "Unless you change and become like little children, you will never enter the kingdom of heaven" (Matthew 18:3). Little children are trusting and usually more concerned with how they feel about things than with what they understand. As adults we need to hold these two things in balance rather than adopting an attitude of intellectual superiority and dismissing our emotions as signs of childish immaturity.

I usually teach by including stories in what I say or write because a true story, based on someone's personal experience, challenges disinterest and intellectual superiority while reinforcing the spiritual message I want to convey. This was how Jesus often taught his disciples and the crowds who came to listen to him. But instead of including stories in *An Invitation to the Spirit-Filled Life*, I've made the decision to rely on the Scriptures to challenge any skeptics. After all,

> The word of God is alive and active. Sharper than any double-edged sword, it penetrates even to dividing soul and spirit, joints and marrow; it judges the thoughts and attitudes of the heart. Nothing in all creation is hidden from God's sight. Everything is uncovered and laid bare before the eyes of him to whom we must give account. (Hebrews 4:12-13)

I've learned that God can speak for himself—we don't have to defend him, only proclaim him. Catholics (for whom this book is mainly but not exclusively written) are for the most part not people of the word. This is the case even though three or four Scripture passages are proclaimed every time we gather to celebrate the Eucharist, Catholic teaching is rooted in Scripture, and Church documents are filled with references to the word of God. In 1976 I fell in love with the word of God—a love that is just as strong today as it was then. My own love for Scripture makes me confident that the word of God can challenge and convict both the heart and mind of every reader of this book as it reveals the person and work of the Holy Spirit in amazing new ways: "Your word is a lamp for my feet, / and a light on my path" (Psalm 119:105). If I am correct, it follows that there is little need here for anecdotes and personal illustrations.

In Catholic understanding, God's revelation comes to us through Scripture and Tradition, the twin foundations on which the teaching of the Church is based. Scripture is the account of God's relationship with his people, which reaches its climax in the mission of his Son, Jesus Christ, and includes the fascinating story of the early years in the lives of the first Christian communities. The Bible is not just one book—it's a library of life-changing books written by human authors who used their natural abilities but were inspired and guided by the Holy Spirit. What we know as the Old and New Testaments were brought together by scholars of the early church in a place called "Biblius" in Lebanon—hence the name "Bible."

Tradition, for its part, is the lived experience of the members of the Christian community since the time of Jesus, based on their reflections on Scripture and the teaching of the apostles and handed down to us through successive generations of bishops of the Church—the successors of the apostles. All this accumulated wisdom is interpreted through the teaching authority vested in the bishops and the magisterium under the guidance of the Holy Spirit. This authority is not superior to the word of God but its servant—it exists to protect the Scriptures from erroneous interpretation and to ensure correct teaching. All the preaching of the Church is to be ruled by Sacred Scripture and Tradition, so it is on the written word of God and the teaching of the apostles and their successors that our faith rests today.

By focusing these reflections on a scriptural presentation of the person and work of the Holy Spirit, my hope is that they will not only be accessible to everyone—all you need is a Bible, a notebook, and a little time—but also easy to follow and understand. In these pages I will, therefore, be quoting Scripture passages more than any other source to show what the Bible reveals to us about the Holy Spirit.

Unless otherwise stated, I will be using the New International Version. I do so because more and more people from all denominations are using this scholarly but user-friendly text. I will also refer to the *Catechism of the Catholic Church*, and sometimes I'll make reference to one of the official documents or encyclicals of the Church or to the words of recent popes, as well as to the early Church Fathers and some prominent Protestant writers. When our understanding of the Holy Spirit rests on the promises of Scripture and on the teaching of the Church, we can face anyone criticizing us with confidence and assurance.

In 1979 I decided to present the teaching on the Holy Spirit by answering a number of frequently asked questions, as this helps to keep a focus on the main issues. Little has changed. I am still asked the same questions, and I still give the same answers. I try to do so in a very straightforward and uncomplicated way. I hope you find this to be true as you read *An Invitation to the Spirit-Filled Life.*

So here at last is this book, presented to you with the added benefit of whatever wisdom I have acquired over the years of "walking the walk." I have tried to write in a way that is accessible to everyone, and this means I may have oversimplified some complex theological issues. It's quite short and can be read like any other book, but the style and approach I have adopted is also that of a study guide, which has the advantage that it can also be used as an individual or group Scripture study on the person and work of the Holy Spirit. This is why each chapter concludes with some Scripture passages and questions for discussion or personal reflection.

The thoughts in the following pages were put together over a number of weeks as the basis for a series of teachings on the Holy Spirit given to our prayer group in Chalfont St. Peter. I make no claim to be anything more than an ordinary Christian to whom God has been gracious enough to reveal himself in a new and wonderful way through the ministry of the Holy Spirit. I owe a deep debt of gratitude to many Christian writers, teachers, and preachers, whose ministries have contributed so much to what is contained in the following pages, and to the many people I have met since 1976 whose lives bear ample witness to the work of the Holy Spirit in our midst. I submit the following pages in humility and love, praying that they may in some part be helpful in opening doors that are still closed and allowing the Holy Spirit to enter and carry out his wonderful work in our lives.

This simple resource is no more than an attempt to explain the One who is our amazing friend, helper, and guide through life: the Father-glorifying, Jesus-revealing, sin-exposing, joy-giving, love-imparting, relationship-building, holiness-encouraging, energy-releasing, truth-telling, witness-enabling, gift-bearing, miracle-working, fruit-producing, power-providing, life-changing, incomparable, and indispensable third person of the Trinity: God the Holy Spirit!

Charles Whitehead

CHAPTER ONE

The Person of the Holy Spirit

1. Who is the Holy Spirit?
2. Is there a clear distinction between the Father, Son, and Holy Spirit?
3. Is the Holy Spirit less important than the Father and the Son?
4. How personal and how present to us is the Holy Spirit?
5. Are we giving too much emphasis to the Holy Spirit?

1. Who is the Holy Spirit?

Many of us begin by thinking of the Spirit as an influence: intangible, present around us, perhaps producing a warm feeling, but somehow unreal. We used to call him the "Holy Ghost," thereby contributing to an impression that he was not really a person, and we reinforced this by often using the impersonal pronoun "it" when referring to him. This made it very unlikely that we would visualize the Holy Spirit as a person.

The Father is clearer to us. Artists portray him in human form and we are familiar with human fathers, so it is much easier to think of him as a person. Jesus, the Son, is also clearly a person; in the Gospels we read of him living among ordinary people and doing many of the same things we do. We are surrounded by images of Jesus: every time we enter a Catholic church, we see him hanging on the cross. So most of us do not have difficulty with the persons of the Father or the Son. But the Spirit? It's hard to recognize him as a person because we have no image of him in human form.

In the Bible the Holy Spirit is described at different times as wind, fire, cloud, water, oil, breath, and light. At the baptism of Jesus, he descends in the form of a dove, which is how he is usually depicted in religious art. "When all the people were being baptized, Jesus was baptized too. And as he was praying, heaven was opened and the Holy Spirit descended on him in bodily form like a dove" (Luke 3:21-22).

But even if none of the above scriptural symbols help us to see the Spirit as a person, it's important to take a brief look to discover what each may reveal about the attributes of the Holy Spirit.

The *dove* is a symbol of peace, love, and gentleness, and it is free to fly wherever it chooses—a good image for the Holy Spirit. After the great flood, Noah released a dove to fly over the waters "to see if the waters had receded from the surface of the ground" (Genesis 8:8). This reminds us of the beginning of the creation story in Genesis 1:2: "And the Spirit of God was hovering over the waters."

Wind can be powerful, destroying, and challenging, or gentle, light, enjoyable, refreshing, and hardly noticeable. This reminds us that the Spirit comes to us in many different ways, including a mighty wind or a gentle breeze. As Jesus said, "The wind blows wherever it pleases. You hear its sound, but you cannot tell where it comes from or where it is going. So it is with everyone born of the Spirit" (John 3:8).

Fire suggests heat, energy, and power, or cleansing and destruction. The fire of the Spirit will cleanse and energize us. As John the Baptist said of Jesus, "I baptize you with water for repentance. But after me comes one who is more powerful than I, whose sandals I am not worthy to carry. He will baptize you with the Holy Spirit and fire" (Matthew 3:11). Fire is a sign of God's presence: think of Moses and the burning bush (Exodus 3) and the pillar of fire (13:21), as well as Elijah at Mount Carmel and the fire from heaven (1 Kings 18). The writer to the Hebrews reminds us, "Our 'God is a consuming fire'" (12:29).

Clouds are mysterious, always moving; they hide things, which are then suddenly revealed. They may be soft and gentle or overshadowing and obscuring. As the *Catechism of the Catholic Church* explains, "The cloud, now obscure, now luminous, reveals the living and saving God, while veiling the transcendence of his glory" (697). This is true of Moses on Mount Sinai (Exodus 24:15-18), at the tent of meeting (33:9-10), during the wandering in the desert (40:36-38), and at the dedication of the Temple (1 Kings 8:10-12). The Spirit comes upon Mary and "the power of the Most High" overshadows her (Luke 1:35). At the transfiguration, the cloud covers Jesus and the three disciples (9:34-35); at his ascension (Acts 1:9), a cloud hides Jesus until the time he will come again in a cloud with great glory (Luke 21:27).

Water is refreshing, cleansing, and life-giving. A place with no water is a desert. Water is essential for all life, and the Spirit is the water of our spiritual life. "Jesus stood and said in a loud voice, 'Let anyone who is thirsty come to me and drink. Whoever believes in me, as Scripture has said, rivers of living water will flow from within them.' By this he meant the Spirit, whom those who believed in him were later to receive" (John 7:37-39).

Oil: We can cook with oil, produce light, and soothe our tired bodies. In Scripture, oil is used for anointing, for consecration to God's service (reminding us of the sacraments), for healing, and for sealing. When Samuel goes to the house of Jesse to anoint David as the future king of Israel, the Lord says, "Rise and anoint him; this is the one" (1 Samuel 16:12). Jesus himself declared, "The Spirit of the Lord is on me, / because he has anointed me" (Luke 4:18). And Paul reminds us that "you were marked in him with a seal, the promised Holy Spirit, who is a deposit guaranteeing our inheritance" (Ephesians 1:13-14).

Breath: When we are breathing, it shows that we are alive— breath is essential for our natural life. "The LORD God . . . breathed into his nostrils the breath of life, and the man became a living being"(Genesis 2:7). In just the same way, the Holy Spirit is essential for our spiritual life: "And with that he [Jesus] breathed on them and said, 'Receive the Holy Spirit'" (John 20:22).

Light: We need light in order to see both naturally and spiritually. God himself is described as light: "God is light; in him there is no darkness at all." (1 John 1:5). We were "called . . . out of darkness into his wonderful light" (1 Peter 2:9), and the psalmist also reminds us, "The LORD is my light" (27:1). We know that this light comes to us through the presence of the Holy Spirit of God in us, which is why Jesus encourages us, "Let your light shine before others, that they may see your good deeds and glorify your Father in heaven" (Matthew 5:16). The Holy Spirit shines God's light into our hearts and minds.

Each of these different symbols tells us something important about the Holy Spirit and offers us clues to the ways in which he will work in our lives.

It is vital, however, from the standpoint of our attitude toward him, to know that the Holy Spirit is a divine person just as much as Jesus and the Father, and therefore he is worthy to receive our love, adoration, and worship. The Holy Spirit is someone in whom we can trust and put our faith. We must not see the Spirit as just a remote channel of power that we in our weakness must plug into and use, but as a person with infinite wisdom, holiness, and tenderness whom we need to invite to be actively involved in our lives, working in us and through us. The Greek word "paraclete," often used to describe the Spirit, means one who is by our side to help us.

We need to develop a relationship with the Holy Spirit. Those who have come to know him as a person will testify that he is not just a warm feeling but an ever-present loving friend and helper, a counselor and advocate, as promised by Jesus: "I will ask the Father, and he will give you another advocate to help you and be with you forever—the Spirit of truth" (John 14:16-17). As St. Paul explains, "Don't you know that you yourselves are God's temple and that God's Spirit dwells in your midst?" (1 Corinthians 3:16).

In the *Catechism*, the Church expresses this relationship in these words: "By sending his only Son and the Spirit of Love in the fullness of time, God has revealed his innermost secret: God himself is an eternal exchange of love, Father, Son, and Holy Spirit, and he has destined us to share in that exchange" (221).

Every time we recite the Creed, we remind ourselves that the Holy Spirit "proceeds from the Father and the Son" and that, together with them, he "is adored and glorified." We know too that we do not just receive the Spirit when we are baptized and confirmed but that he is constantly being poured out, proceeding from God who is always giving him to equip us for life as Christians: "For God did not call us to be impure, but to live a holy life. Therefore, anyone who rejects this instruction does not reject a human being but God, . . . who gives you his Holy Spirit" (1 Thessalonians 4:7-8).

When we begin to see the Holy Spirit as a person in his own right who wants to be in relationship with us, we will be more open to a change in our approach to him, and the process of transforming our lives can begin.

2. Is there a clear distinction in the Bible between the Father, the Son, and the Holy Spirit?

Yes, there are clear distinctions between the three persons, and it is evident that they each have quite distinct personalities. They have a definite relationship with each other, they speak of and to one another, and they have particular roles and work to do; at the same time, they are in total unity.

- In Luke 3:21-22, when Jesus is baptized by John, there is a clear distinction between Jesus who comes out of the water, the Father who speaks affirming words from heaven, and the Spirit who descends upon Jesus in the form of a dove.

- In John 14:16, when Jesus tells his disciples about the coming of the Spirit, there is again a clear distinction between Jesus who will ask, the Father who will answer, and the Spirit of truth who will be given as the answer: "And I will ask the Father, and he will give you another advocate to help you and be with you forever."

- In Matthew 28:19-20, the last words Jesus speaks to his disciples clearly identify the three distinct persons of God: "Therefore go and make disciples of all nations, baptizing them in the name of the Father and of the Son and of the Holy Spirit, and teaching them to obey everything I have commanded you."

- In Acts 2:33, Peter explains to the crowds gathered in Jerusalem for Pentecost what it is that they have just experienced: "Exalted to the right hand of God, he [Jesus] has received from the Father the promised Holy Spirit and has poured out what you now see and hear."

- Finally, in John 16:5-16, Jesus tells his followers that he must go back to the Father but that the Spirit will come in his place to be with them: "Now I am going to him who sent me. . . . Unless I go away, the Advocate will not come to you; . . . but when he, the Spirit of truth, comes, he will guide you into all the truth" (verses 5, 7, 13).

In the *Catechism of the Catholic Church*, we are reminded that

the One whom the Father has sent into our hearts, the Spirit of his Son, is truly God. Consubstantial with the Father and the Son, the Spirit is inseparable from them. . . . When the Father sends his Word, he always sends his Breath. In their joint mission, the Son and the Holy Spirit are distinct but inseparable. . . . It is Christ who is seen, the visible image of the invisible God, but it is the Spirit who reveals him. (689)

So although the doctrine of the Trinity is not directly and specifically taught in Scripture, it is accepted by putting together a number of facts that are clearly taught. From these we know there is one God, but there are three distinct, equal, and divine persons in this one God—the Father, the Son, and the Holy Spirit. Karl Rahner's book *The Trinity*, which caused a stir among other theologians when it was first published in 1970, expressed the view that despite professing belief in the Trinity, many Christians give very little thought to the three distinct persons in the Godhead. In Rahner 's words, "Should the doctrine of the Trinity have to be dropped as false, the major part of religious literature could well remain virtually unchanged."[1]

Perhaps we need to ask ourselves if, in practice, the doctrine of the Trinity really makes any difference to the lives of most Christians. This may help explain why so many people rarely think about the personality of the Holy Spirit or the clearly defined work he wants to do in their lives.

3. Is the Holy Spirit less important than the Father and Jesus?

While the answer to this question is definitely no, it's easy to understand why someone would ask it. When we look at the number of theological books written on the Trinity, we quickly see that a relatively small proportion of them is devoted to the Holy Spirit. When I ask people which are the most important Christian feast days, I always hear about Christmas and Easter but only occasionally about Pentecost.

In my school days, apart from the weeks preceding my confirmation, I can hardly remember any systematic teaching on the Holy Spirit. All these things may, therefore, cause us to ask whether the Spirit is less important, less than equal, and, in some strange way, less divine than God the Father and God the Son. Of course, this is nonsense; the three persons of God are equal in every way. But how are we to present a clear picture of the Holy Spirit to make clear his equality and importance?

Scripture tells us that the Holy Spirit has four divine attributes:

- He is eternal: "Through the eternal Spirit . . . " (Hebrews 9:14).
- He is omnipresent: "Where can I go from your Spirit?" (Psalm 139:7).
- He is omnipotent: "You will receive power when the Holy Spirit comes on you" (Acts 1:8).
- He is omniscient: "He [the Spirit] will guide you into all the truth" (John 16:13).

And he carries out three divine works:

- He creates: "The Spirit of God was hovering over the waters" (Genesis 1:2).
- He gives life: "The Spirit gives life" (John 6:63).
- He inspires prophecy: "Prophets, though human, spoke from God as they were carried along by the Holy Spirit." (2 Peter 1:21).

Scripture also shows us that his name is coupled with those of the Father and the Son in a way that expresses full equality and divinity: "May the grace of the Lord Jesus Christ, and the love of God, and the fellowship of the Holy Spirit be with you all" (2 Corinthians 13:14). And in Acts 5:3-4, when Peter addresses Ananias, he speaks of lying to the Holy Spirit and lying to God as being one and the same, saying, "You have lied to the Holy Spirit. . . . You have not lied just to human beings but to God."

From these simple examples of the divine attributes, the divine works, the linking of the Spirit with the Father and the Son, and the fact that he is called God, we can see that the Holy Spirit is a person, distinct from the Father and Son, but fully and equally divine. He cannot, therefore, be any less important. So it is entirely appropriate to worship and adore him, to pray to and through him, and to enter into a living and dynamic relationship with him. For those who may wish to look into this in greater depth, I suggest

- a study of the Holy Spirit in the *Catechism of the Catholic Church* (687–716);

- a look at the writings of Pope St. John Paul II on the Holy Spirit, including his encyclical *Dominum et Vivificantem* (On the Holy Spirit in the Life of the Church and the World);
- a Bible study of the numerous references to the Spirit in the Old and New Testaments, including Joel 2:28-29 and John 14–16.

Here are three helpful insights offered by St. Augustine into the Holy Spirit:

- he is the unifying love and communion in the Trinity;
- he is the love that persists and lasts;
- he is both the Giver and the Gift.[2]

Should we be thinking of the Holy Spirit in the same way we think of Jesus and therefore behave toward him as a loving, wise, and tender person? Yes, I'm sure that we should! In the Gospel of John, Jesus tells his disciples that he will not leave them orphans and that the Spirit will come to them in his place (14:16-18). They must have wondered how anyone, no less an unknown Holy Spirit, could possibly be anything like Jesus. They were to find out on the day of Pentecost.

4. How personal and how present to us is the Holy Spirit?

He has personal characteristics:

- He has knowledge: "No one knows the thoughts of God except the Spirit of God" (1 Corinthians 2:11).
- He has will: "He [the Spirit] distributes them to each one, just as he determines" (1 Corinthians 12:11).
- He loves: "By the love of the Spirit . . . " (Romans 15:30).
- He grieves: "Do not grieve the Holy Spirit of God" (Ephesians 4:30).

He acts as a person:

- He searches: "The Spirit searches all things, even the deep things of God" (1 Corinthians 2:10).
- He speaks: "The Holy Spirit spoke . . . through David" (Acts 1:16).
- He calls out: "The Spirit . . . calls out, '*Abba*, Father'" (Galatians 4:6).
- He intercedes: "The Spirit himself intercedes for us" (Romans 8:26).
- He teaches: "The Holy Spirit . . . will teach you all things" (John 14:26).
- He leads: "Those who are led by the Spirit of God are the children of God" (Romans 8:14).
- He commands: "The Spirit told Philip . . . " (Acts 8:29).
- He appoints: " . . . all the flock of which the Holy Spirit has made you overseers" (Acts 20:28).
- He forbids: "The Spirit of Jesus would not allow them to" (Acts 16:7).

He is treated as a person:

- He is rebelled against: "Yet they rebelled / and grieved his Holy Spirit" (Isaiah 63:10).
- He is insulted: "Who has insulted the Spirit of grace?" (Hebrews 10:29).
- He is lied to: "You have lied to the Holy Spirit" (Acts 5:3).
- He is blasphemed against: "Blasphemy against the Spirit will not be forgiven" (Matthew 12:31).
- He is resisted: "You always resist the Holy Spirit!" (Acts 7:51).

We can also notice that in every translation of the Bible, the personal pronoun "he" is used when referring to the Holy Spirit, a practice I am following in this book.

He has a particular work to do:

- He creates: "The Spirit of God has made me" (Job 33:4).
- He witnesses: "We are witnesses of these things, and so is the Holy Spirit" (Acts 5:32).
- He convicts of sin: "He will prove the world to be in the wrong about sin" (John 16:8).
- He makes us new: "He [God] saved us through the washing of rebirth and renewal by the Holy Spirit" (Titus 3:5).
- He sets us free: "The law of the Spirit who gives life has set you free" (Romans 8:2).
- He strengthens us: "May [he] strengthen you with power through his Spirit" (Ephesians 3:16).

- He leads us: "Those who are led by the Spirit of God are the children of God" (Romans 8:14).
- He produces fruit: "The fruit of the Spirit is love, joy, peace . . . " (Galatians 5:22-23).
- He supports all believers: "The Spirit is given for the common good" (1 Corinthians 12:7).
- He distributes gifts: "There are different kinds of gifts, but the same Spirit distributes them. . . . In everyone it is the same God at work" (1 Corinthians 12:4, 6).
- He protects us: "Having been kept by the Holy Spirit from preaching the word in Asia . . . " (Acts 16:6).
- He reminds us: "The Holy Spirit . . . will remind you of everything I have said to you" (John 14:26).

These are just some examples, and we can find many other ways in which the Holy Spirit is at work. But above all, his purpose is to reveal Jesus to us, and in order to ensure that Jesus is lifted up, he makes himself less conspicuous. Perhaps this is one of the reasons we lose sight of his work, his power, his authority, and his importance.

So far in this chapter, we have seen that the Holy Spirit is a person, distinct from but coequal with the Father and Son. He has a particular and necessary work to do in each one of us, but he will wait until we invite him to come to us and take control of our lives. When he comes, he will reveal Jesus as a living Lord in a wonderful new way.

So often the excitement of the present-day, miracle-working Lord is missing because our eyes are fixed on what happened during the earthly ministry of Jesus. So we have no real concept of a living, contemporary Lord, present in our lives and wanting to work through us to reach out and touch those around us. Through the ministry of the Holy Spirit, many are discovering this glorious experience anew. It is the Spirit's desire to come to us as a loving friend and helper so that he can point us to the living Jesus as Lord and to God as our loving Father. As St. Paul reminds us, "No one can say, 'Jesus is Lord,' except by the Holy Spirit" (1 Corinthians 12:3) and "The Spirit himself testifies with our spirit that we are God's children" (Romans 8:16).

If we allow him, the Spirit will securely anchor us in these two key relationships. He is the Spirit of unity, and we really need to know him well and allow him to work in us and through us. But unless we believe in him—knowing that when we ask, he will be given—we will never ask, and so we will not experience his life-changing presence.

5. Are we now giving too much emphasis to the Holy Spirit?

This is a cause of concern for some people, and perhaps in order to correct a deficiency, a need has been felt to overcompensate. But the Spirit himself always points us to Jesus and the Father. The Holy Spirit is like a spotlight, and we should certainly not be gazing into the spotlight but at the ones on whom the light falls. If we stare into the spotlight, we become dazzled and unable to see clearly, but we do need the spotlight to focus our attention on the full wonder and glory of the person of Jesus and to help us see God as our loving Father.

Without the Holy Spirit freely at work in us, our understanding of Jesus and the Father will remain limited, and we will find ourselves trying to live the Christian life without the power that God provides to make it possible. Because the Holy Spirit does not draw attention to himself, someone must do it for him; otherwise, he may well be overlooked. One of God's purposes of the great outpourings of the Holy Spirit that began in the twentieth century and continues today is to demonstrate the life-changing effects of a new experience of the love and activity of the Holy Spirit. This has been revealed to us in grassroots explosions of supernatural power in millions of men and women all over the world.

To look at this in another way, there are Christians who know they have Jesus beside them, and there are others who know they must be *in* Jesus, with his life inside of them through the presence of the Holy Spirit. Those in the first group try to handle the problems of life with their own strength, with an occasional prayer for divine help, whereas those in the second group knows that on their own they are helpless. However, they also know that with the person and presence of God living in them through the Holy Spirit, heavenly power has come to earth and will be effective if they surrender to it. They have understood they must be in Jesus:

> "Remain in me, as I also remain in you. No branch can bear fruit by itself; it must remain in the vine. Neither can you bear fruit unless you remain in me. I am the vine; you are the branches. If you remain in me and I in you, you will bear much fruit; apart from me you can do nothing." (John 15:4-5)

This second group of people know that their lives are now in Christ and that the Holy Spirit living in them is the sign and guarantee of this truth. The inside life, us in Jesus and Jesus in us, is what the Holy Spirit will bring about in each of us—if we allow him to. He will not force himself upon us, but our clear YES will mean that his power is released within us and that we are filled with the utter fullness of God. We need to clearly teach about the vital role of the Holy Spirit in the life of every Christian because so many people have not understood the fullness and power available to them through the Holy Spirit. We must bring about a proper balance in our appreciation of the importance and work of all three persons of the Trinity: Father, Son, and Spirit.

Above all, the working of the Spirit in us must be visible to others. We have to embody the message and the experience, to be living examples. Why is this important? Because "modern man listens more willingly to witnesses than to teachers, and if he does listen to teachers, it is because they are witnesses," said Blessed Pope Paul VI.[3]

But even if we have been baptized and confirmed, we may still be unaware of the need to personally and deliberately invite the Holy Spirit to be at work in our lives. We have to ask, as Jesus tells us:

> "So I say to you: Ask and it will be given to you; seek and you will find; knock and the door will be opened to you. For everyone who asks receives; the one who seeks finds; and to the one who knocks, the door will be opened. Which of you fathers, if your son asks for a fish, will give him a snake instead? Or if he asks for an egg, will give him a scorpion? If you then, though you are evil, know how to give good gifts

to your children, how much more will your Father in heaven give the Holy Spirit to those who ask him!" (Luke 11:9-13)

How all this relates to our baptism and confirmation will be addressed in the coming chapters, but in the above Scripture passage, Jesus is making it very clear: the Holy Spirit is the good gift our Father longs to give us, but the gift is given "to those who ask him" (Luke 11:13). Why do we need the gift? Because there is work to be done that only the Holy Spirit can do.

Sadly, so many are unaware of this truth. There is a real need today to talk about the person and work of the Spirit so that people will find a new desire to live a fuller life in the Holy Spirit. Perhaps, then, more and more will decide to "ask," discovering, to their great surprise, that when they do, they receive the Holy Spirit in an amazing new way. But if we are like the disciples that Paul encountered at Ephesus, who "have not even heard that there is a Holy Spirit" (Acts 19:2), or if we have never understood that the gift of the Holy Spirit has been given, we won't even know we can ask for it. We need to give more emphasis to the Holy Spirit in order to correct the weaknesses and ignorance that have crept into the understanding of so many in the Church today, thereby undermining his work in our lives.

When God makes promises, he keeps them—think of Abram, Mary, or Peter. He has given us himself in the person of Jesus, and where Jesus is, his Spirit is also—the two are "conjoined and inseparable," as the *Catechism* expresses it (743; cf. 689). In the words of Jesus in the Book of Revelation, "'Come!' Let the one who is thirsty come; and let the one who wishes take the free gift of the water of life" (22:17). This water of life is the Holy Spirit, a gift freely offered to all who will accept him. *Come, Holy Spirit!*

Questions For Reflection and Discussion

1. Jesus tells us that the Holy Spirit, poured out on Pentecost, is a person to whom we can relate. We may know *about* him, but do we really *know* him?

2. The Holy Spirit is God and is therefore to be loved, worshipped, glorified, and adored. Do you see him as a divine person with whom you can have a personal relationship?

3. The Holy Spirit is quite distinct from the Father and the Son but coequal. What does this mean to you in practice, and how does it affect the way you look upon the Holy Spirit?

4. The Holy Spirit has a vital job to do in the life of every member of the body of Christ. Have you ever deliberately and consciously invited him to work freely in your life? If not, why not?

Helpful Scripture passages to pray:
   John 14:15-31
   Luke 3:21-22
   John 16:5-16
   Luke 11:9-13

CHAPTER TWO

The Promise of the Holy Spirit

1. Where do we find the promise?
2. Who makes the promise?
3. What is promised, and to whom is the promise made?
4. When can we receive the promise?
5. What questions might we ask ourselves to find out whether we need the help of the Holy Spirit?

1. Where do we find the promise?

We first find the promise in the Old Testament. The Old Testament prophets were specially chosen for their ministries, and they and certain priests and kings received the Spirit in part—not the fullness, only a "measure" of the Spirit—to equip them for what God had called them to do. Almost all the prophets pointed to the widespread outpouring of the Holy Spirit that would one day come. They spoke of God giving his people a new heart and a new spirit, but it was only at Pentecost that the Holy Spirit became available to all people in his fullness, just as they had prophesied. Here are a few examples of their prophecies:

- All God's people will one day be empowered by the Spirit: "I will pour out my Spirit on your offspring" (Isaiah 44:3). "And afterward, I will pour out my Spirit on all people" (Joel 2:28). "I will give you a new heart and put a new spirit in you" (Ezekiel 36:26).

- The Messiah will be empowered by the Spirit: "Here is my servant, . . . my chosen one . . . ; I will put my Spirit on him" (Isaiah 42:1).

- The new covenant will be in the Spirit: "I will put my Spirit in you. . . . You will be my people, and I will be your God" (Ezekiel 36:27, 28).

We find the promise repeated and amplified in the New Testament, where it is first fulfilled in Jesus.

- Jesus is conceived by the power of the Holy Spirit: "The Holy Spirit will come on you" (Luke 1:35).

- He is anointed with the Holy Spirit after his baptism by John: "The Holy Spirit descended on him in bodily form like a dove" (Luke 3:22).

- He is led by the Spirit into the desert: "Jesus, full of the Holy Spirit, left the Jordan and was led by the Spirit into the wilderness" (Luke 4:1).

- He comes out of the desert "in the power of the Spirit" (Luke 4:14).

- He demonstrates the power of the Spirit in his public ministry: "By the Spirit of God . . . I drive out demons" (Matthew 12:28).

- John the Baptist, who received the Spirit even before his birth (Luke 1:15) and is described by Jesus as "more than a prophet" (7:26), tells us that in Jesus we not only receive forgiveness and cleansing from sin; through him the fire of the Holy Spirit is released: "He will baptize you with the Holy Spirit and fire" (3:16).

- Jesus promises his disciples that they will receive the Holy Spirit: "I will ask the Father, and he will give you . . . the Spirit of truth" (John 14:16, 17). "When he, the Spirit of truth, comes . . . " (16:13). "The Spirit will receive from me what he will make known to you" (16:15).

2. So who makes the promise?

God our Father makes the promise! The Holy Spirit is the promised gift of the Father, released to us by the work of Jesus. Before we could receive the Spirit, Jesus had to die, rise from the dead, and return to his Father. When Jesus spoke about leaving the disciples in John 16, they were afraid. Their lives revolved around him and his physical presence among them, and so they were unable to imagine what could possibly be better than that. We would almost certainly have felt the same way. They had no idea that they were about to enter a new period of history: the age of the Holy Spirit, the age in which we are now living, when God himself is present in the heart and life of every Christian through the person of the Holy Spirit, given to us on the day of Pentecost.

After Jesus had ascended, the disciples waited in Jerusalem for the Father's gift:

- "Wait for the gift my Father promised" (Acts 1:4).

- "I am going to send you what my Father has promised" (Luke 24:49).

- "When the Advocate comes, whom I will send to you from the Father . . . " (John 15:26).

- "He [Jesus] has received from the Father the promised Holy Spirit" (Acts 2:33).

- "How much more will your Father in heaven give the Holy Spirit to those who ask him!" (Luke 11:13).

Jesus promised that the Spirit, the Helper, would be with us always: "I will ask the Father, and he will give you another advocate to help you and be with you forever—the Spirit of truth" (John 14:16-17). So there is no need to be lonely or afraid, hopeless, or helpless ever again. We are never "orphans" (14:18); the Father and the Son are here in us through the presence of the Holy Spirit. He is with us every moment of our lives, and he is enough—we need nothing more. To put it another way: the glorified Jesus is not just with us but also in us, working from the inside out to transform our lives.

This is what happened on Pentecost Day, when the promise of the Spirit was fulfilled.

3. What is promised, and to whom is the promise made?

The promise is "the Spirit of truth—to be with you forever" (John 16:13; 14:16).

Not
- just a set of gifts;
- a particular experience;
- a warm feeling;
- a religious ritual.

But
- the person;
- the presence;
- the love;
- the power;
- the new life of God himself, released in us here and now in the Spirit.

Why?
- to renew us inwardly and outwardly;
- to renew us in our relationships with God, ourselves, and others;
- to renew us in our Christian witness;
- to make us holy (after all, he is the Holy Spirit!).

So the promise is the gift to us of the Holy Spirit: God himself, to renew and change us, to equip us to live the Christian life.

The promise is made to those who ask! Jesus said, "How much more will your Father in heaven give the Holy Spirit to those who ask him!" (Luke 11:13) and "Anyone who is thirsty, come to me and drink" (John 7:37).

If we have received the Holy Spirit as part of our Christian initiation, why are we exhorted to ask, to come, and to drink? Because we must make a positive and personal response to the gift we've been given—we must say a definitive YES to what we've received. Only then are the love and power of the Spirit within us fully released and effective, and this may not have happened when we were baptized and confirmed.

The promise is to all who repent and are baptized. Peter challenges the crowd on the day of Pentecost, and three thousand people respond, are baptized, and receive the Holy Spirit: "Repent and be baptized, every one of you, in the name of Jesus Christ for the forgiveness of your sins. And you will receive the gift of the Holy Spirit." (Acts 2:38). Repentance and baptism will normally precede the giving of the Holy Spirit: "The promise is for you and your children and for all who are far off—for all whom the Lord our God will call" (2:39). So the promise is made to us when we ask, when we repent, when we are baptized, and when we respond to the Lord's call. It is made

- to us and our children;
- to all who are far off;
- to those the Lord calls.

4. When can we receive the promise?

When we become Christians and are baptized. "Repent and be baptized . . . and you will receive the gift of the Holy Spirit" (Acts 2:38).

When we ask. "After they prayed, . . . they were all filled with the Holy Spirit and spoke the word of God boldly" (Acts 4:31).

When the Father fulfills the promise. The Father poured out "power from on high" (Luke 24:49), and the disciples and many others were "baptized with the Holy Spirit" (Acts 1:5; cf. 1:8; 2:4).

The same promise is later fulfilled for the Gentiles: "While Peter was still speaking these words, the Holy Spirit came on all who heard the message. The circumcised believers [Jews] who had come with Peter were astonished that the gift of the Holy Spirit had been poured out even on Gentiles" (Acts 10:44-45).

When the Church prays. Peter and John were sent down to Samaria, and "when they arrived, they prayed for the new believers there that they might receive the Holy Spirit" (Acts 8:15).

When God heals. In Acts 9:15-19, we read how Ananias is sent to the blind Saul, "so that you may see again and be filled with the Holy Spirit . . . and he [Saul] could see again. He got up and was baptized" (verses 17, 18).

Note that St. Paul assumes that all Christians have received and are availing themselves of the Spirit and his power: "You, however, are not in the realm of the flesh but are in the realm of the Spirit, if indeed the Spirit of God lives in you. And if anyone does not have the Spirit of Christ, they do not belong to Christ" (Romans 8:9). But for many of us, there is still a question to answer—not about receiving, but about availing. Have we thrown open the doors and windows of our lives to the fresh, empowering wind of the Holy Spirit?

The gift to us of the Holy Spirit is the fulfillment of the promise, but with the Holy Spirit there is a "now" and a "not yet." The Spirit has begun in us, and the fact that he has begun is the guarantee of completion. "When you believed, you were marked in him [Christ] with a seal, the promised Holy Spirit, who is a deposit guaranteeing our inheritance" (Ephesians 1:13-14). But if we think of the above text, Romans 8:9, the extent to which we are "in the realm of the Spirit" will depend upon the extent to which we have surrendered our lives to his control. Many of us in whom the Spirit of God lives may not be controlled by the Spirit. That's because there are areas of our lives that we have not yet surrendered. We must give the power back to God in every part of our lives and leave it with him. To do this, we need to be constantly refilled with the Holy Spirit so that we are transformed into the Lord's likeness (cf. 2 Corinthians 3:18).

We receive the promise when we ask! "Let the one who is thirsty come; and let the one who wishes take the free gift of the water of life" (Revelation 22:17). God is the one who gives us everything in creation, but he goes even further and gives us himself. The gift is Jesus and the Spirit of Jesus, and as we saw chapter 1, the two are conjoined and inseparable (*Catechism*, 743). Paul urges all of us to renew our experience of the Holy Spirit, to be filled again and again: "Be filled with the Spirit" (Ephesians 5:18). The use in the original text of the verb "filled" implies that we need to go on being filled, and this was certainly the experience of the early Christian community. For example, we see that as the disciples prayed—only a short time after they were all filled on the day of Pentecost—"they were all filled with the Holy Spirit and spoke the word of God boldly" (Acts 4:31).

It's really important to note that these early disciples continued to pray regularly to be filled again with the Spirit, and so should we. The full release of the Spirit in our lives is not something that happens automatically through our Christian initiation. Yes, we receive the Holy Spirit. But unless our response is wholehearted, the outworking of the grace is restricted, and when our expectation is low, little will happen.

We cannot assume today that because someone has been baptized and confirmed, they are fully alive in the Spirit—this is more likely to be the exception rather than the rule. It's why we regularly need to pray for and receive a new outpouring of the Spirit. This should not be seen as a second blessing but as a recovery of an unrealized part of the original blessing—the grace we received at baptism. I will speak further on this later, in chapter 3 on the baptism in the Holy Spirit.

Jamie Buckingham, a very practical Christian writer, explains how we should understand being filled with the Spirit and why we need to be filled:

At the very moment you were born again, the Holy Spirit took up residence in your life. However, that does not mean you are filled with the Holy Spirit. To be filled means that you are controlled and empowered. It means you are relying on the power of God to change your life, rather than trying to do it yourself. Power for living is yours only when you yield to him and let him control your life. You cannot live the Christian life in your own power through self-determination and self-discipline. Only Jesus was able to live a perfect life, and only as he lives in you through his Spirit can you live victoriously. In a nutshell, to be filled with the Holy Spirit means to be filled with Jesus.[4]

In a conversation I had with him, Cardinal Leon Josef Suenens, one of the key figures of the Second Vatican Council, explained it to me in a very simple way: the question we need to ask ourselves is not "Do I have the Spirit?" because if we've been baptized, we have the Spirit. The question we must ask is, "Does the Spirit have me?" Do I know for certain that I have clearly and unequivocally given him permission to be in control and to direct my life? Did I even realize that I'm supposed to do that? If not, I need to do it without delay.

Many of us had to wait to experience the fullness of the Holy Spirit until we had been Christians for many years. So could we have received all that was available at the time of our conversion to Christ or at our initiation into the Church?

Yes, we could have, and we did. But we didn't understand the fullness of what we had received because no one had taught us or told us, so we didn't expect much to happen. Or perhaps we were told but lacked the faith to fully receive what God was giving. If only we had believed in the streams of living water that Jesus speaks of (John 7:37-39), we could have moved from living on spiritual snacks to enjoying lavish banquets years ago! The Holy Spirit really is the Church's best-kept secret. If we ask what the Church needs most, the answer must be "the power of the Holy Spirit."

Blessed Pope Paul VI's answer was unequivocal: "The Spirit, the Holy Spirit, . . . the Church needs her perennial Pentecost; she needs fire in her heart, words on her lips, prophecy in her outlook."[5] Some will remember the prayer Pope St. John XXIII asked the whole Church to pray before the opening of the Second Vatican Council: "Renew your wonders in this day as by a new Pentecost!"

How will the Church experience a new Pentecost? When most baptized people are fully alive in the grace of the sacrament, empowered for discipleship, and open to the Holy Spirit each and every day.

If we want to have the fullness of the Holy Spirit alive and active in us, we need to pray frequently to be filled again with this grace. Why? Because the distractions of daily living, the sins we commit, and the pressures of circumstances—of other people's demands and needs and the events over which we have no control—weaken the effectiveness of the Holy Spirit in us, causing us to lose our focus on living in his love and power. So we need to pray again, "Come, Holy Spirit!" When we do this, he comes and fills us again.

As I noted previously, on the day of Pentecost, the disciples were all "filled with the Holy Spirit" (Acts 2:4), but later, "they were all filled with the Holy Spirit and spoke the word of God boldly" (4:31). They needed this fresh filling with the Spirit, and so do we! In the next chapter, we will be looking at the meaning and purpose of baptism in the Holy Spirit. But even before we do that, it's important to recognize that we will always need regular prayer for fresh outpourings of the Holy Spirit. Just like the early disciples of Jesus, we, too, need to be refilled regularly with the Spirit. We must never feel discouraged by this; we simply need to come to the Lord regularly, asking him to fill us again with his Holy Spirit.

When we meet with other brothers and sisters in the Lord, we should always take the opportunity to ask for a fresh outpouring of the Holy Spirit. The Church constantly prays, "Come, Holy Spirit!" and so should we. It's simply a matter of laying hands on someone in faith and asking Jesus to fill that person again with his Holy Spirit—nothing complicated or strange, just a simple prayer. In this way, we will stay fully alive in the grace of our baptism and confirmation and be open to the prompting and guidance of the Holy Spirit day by day. This is the way it's supposed to be; this is God's provision to equip us to live effective and fruitful Christian lives in the midst of our challenging and frequently confusing world.

Come, Holy Spirit!

5. What questions might we ask ourselves to find out whether we need the help of the Holy Spirit?

The series of questions below is designed to reveal to you how much evidence there is of the Spirit's presence and work in your life. The references to the Scripture passages will help you understand how you might recognize this.

The Holy Spirit was promised in the Old Testament, revealed in the life of Jesus, and poured out on the infant church on Pentecost. He is the gift of God our Father and is available in his fullness to all who ask—and that obviously includes you!

- What evidence is there of the Spirit's work in my life? (Romans 8:5)
- Am I ever aware of the inner prompting of the Holy Spirit? (Acts 16:6-8)
- Is Jesus real to me as a person and as my Lord? (1 Peter 3:15)
- Am I secure in my relationship as a child of the Father? (Romans 8:15-16)
- Do I see in myself a love for other people, and do I have a concern and care for people I would not normally choose as friends? (1 John 4:11-12)
- Do I find there are times when words I am saying really touch and help someone with a problem? (1 Corinthians 12:8)
- Am I ready to talk to others about my Christian faith? (Matthew 10:8)
- Do I receive help when I pray? (Romans 8:26-27)
- Is there a new excitement when I read the Bible? (Hebrews 4:12-13)
- Is there a new freedom in praising and worshipping God? (Ephesians 1:3-14)

- Is the Eucharist at the center of my spiritual life? (1 Corinthians 11:23-26; *Catechism,* 1324)
- Am I growing in holiness, which St. John Paul II called "the essential prerequisite for an authentic evangelization?"[6]
- Do I feel a need to put on the full armor of God? (Ephesians 6:12-18)
- Am I exercising any of the spiritual gifts? (1 Corinthians 12:7)
- Is the fruit of the Spirit evident in my life? (Galatians 5:22-23)
- Am I playing an active part in the life of my local church? (Acts 2:46-47)
- Have I ever really asked God for his gift, for the fullness of the Holy Spirit? (Luke 11:9-13)

CHAPTER THREE

Baptism in the Holy Spirit

1. Why do we talk about being "baptized in the Holy Spirit," and how does it relate to our baptism and confirmation?
2. How do we describe baptism in the Holy Spirit?
3. How can we receive this new life in the Spirit?
4. Are there any hindrances to receiving it?
5. What is likely to happen after we have received this gift from God?
6. How can we pray for someone to be baptized in the Holy Spirit?

We have seen that the Holy Spirit is a person in his own right, the gift of the Father released to us by Jesus, and he comes to us at the time of our Christian initiation. Subsequent to this, he also comes, whenever we ask him, as a friend and helper, equipping and empowering us to live the Christian life. In doing so, he reveals Jesus as a living Lord and Savior and God as our loving Father. He is the source of the new life that will transform us, and all we have to do is ask him to come. When this happens, we may say that we have been "baptized in the Spirit," using the phrase we find in several places in the New Testament.

People often speak of "the baptism in the Spirit," a phrase not found in the Scriptures but one that is generally accepted and in common usage, as it is of course directly derived from the phrase "baptized in the Spirit." But in my opinion, it is probably better to avoid using "the," as this suggests a unique event, whereas the Lord may pour out his Spirit upon us time and again. Since being filled with the Spirit should be an ongoing experience, it fits well to use the verb form "baptized" in the Spirit, which is active and dynamic. But in nearly all the English-speaking world, the most often used phrase is "baptism in the Spirit," whereas in France, Italy, and Spain, the normal descriptions are *effusion de l'Esprit, effusione dello Spirito*, and *efusion del Espiritu*, all of which we would probably translate as "outpouring of the Spirit."

In this chapter, we will consider the relationship between baptism in water and baptism in the Spirit, explained in these words by St. Augustine: "The Spirit is promised not only to him who does not have but also to him who already has. For it is given to one who has not, in order that he may have; and to the one who has, that he may have more abundantly."[7] On June 1, 2014, Pope Francis addressed a gathering of more than fifty thousand Catholic charismatics in Rome at the Olympic Stadium and told them, "I expect you to share with everyone in the Church the grace of baptism in the Holy Spirit."[8]

1. Why do we talk about being "baptized in the Holy Spirit," and how does it relate to our baptism and confirmation?

We talk about being baptized in the Holy Spirit because the phrase is used in the New Testament by John the Baptist and by Jesus himself:

> John answered them all, "I baptize you with water. But one who is more powerful than I will come. . . . He will baptize you with the Holy Spirit and fire." (Luke 3:16)

> Jesus told his disciples, "For John baptized with water, but in a few days you will be baptized with the Holy Spirit." (Acts 1:5)

We see what Jesus means by this most clearly in the account of the coming of the Holy Spirit to Jesus' disciples on the day of Pentecost. They were all filled with the Spirit and completely transformed:

> Suddenly a sound like the blowing of a violent wind came from heaven and filled the whole house where they were sitting. They saw what seemed to be tongues of fire that separated and came to rest on each of them. All of them were filled with the Holy Spirit and began to speak in other tongues as the Spirit enabled them. (Acts 2:1-4)

We look to Pentecost as the birthday of the Church. The disciples were no longer just a group of individual followers of Jesus; they were now a community with a mission. The immediate result is clearly evident in Peter, who fearlessly and confidently preached an amazing sermon, resulting in three thousand converts to Christianity (Acts 2:41). The rough, tough, ignorant fisherman had been transformed into a preacher whose every word was filled with conviction and passion. Today we may debate how to describe what happens when we receive the Holy Spirit, when and how it should occur, and what we should call it. But we can never doubt that something life-changing is supposed to happen that in many ways will resemble the experience of the first disciples at Pentecost.

When we are baptized, whether as babies or as adults, we receive the Holy Spirit, and our Christian initiation is completed with a special coming of the Spirit at our confirmation. There is no disagreement about this, and on neither occasion do we normally hear people speak about being baptized in the Holy Spirit. But when someone subsequently makes a special act of surrendering himself to the Holy Spirit, inviting the Spirit to take control of his life, and a change in the person is very quickly evident, we do speak of that person as being baptized in the Holy Spirit. This is what we are trying to address—what happens, and how do we explain it?

There are two schools of thought about baptism in the Holy Spirit, and I think there are good arguments for both. I'm not a theologian, and I don't see that the two views are mutually exclusive but rather complementary.

God is sovereign, and he often acts outside the boundaries we try to lay down. Many people have experienced dramatic changes in their lives after they have been prayed with for baptism in the Holy Spirit. They attribute these changes to that specific prayer because they recognize that there is a new power at work in them and through them, helping them to live out their Christian lives with greater commitment and effectiveness. The experience happens, and the theological explanations follow.

A release of sacramental grace

The first school of thought is that baptism in the Holy Spirit is a release of sacramental graces. It is a release of the graces received through the sacraments of Christian initiation: baptism and confirmation. But why does the grace need to be released? It's an accepted view that the grace of the sacraments received is always present, but sometimes it is restricted. In other words, this grace is present in us but constrained, not able to work freely and not, therefore, as effective as it could and should be. Why? Because we, the recipients, have not responded as we should.

Most of us were baptized as infants, before we were capable of believing anything, and it is quite possible that since then we have never personally and fully accepted the Christian commitment made on our behalf by our parents and godparents. When we later received the Sacrament of Confirmation, we again quite likely lacked any deep personal commitment to the Lord or to living a full Christian life in the power of the Spirit. So we never realized that we are called first to be disciples of Jesus, and then we are sent out in the power of the Spirit to "make disciples of all nations" (Matthew 28:19).

In fact, there is little point in going out in response to the Church's call for a new evangelization if we have not first come to Jesus to receive his new life and then been empowered and equipped by his Holy Spirit. Those who have been "sacramentalized" but not evangelized are simply not equipped to play their part in an evangelizing Church. Our empowering for mission comes when we embrace the sacraments of our Christian initiation and open ourselves to the outpouring of the charismatic gifts, freely given as the Spirit decides (1 Corinthians 12:11; *Lumen Gentium*, 12), to be used for the benefit of others. There is an important link between a new Pentecost and a new evangelization—the former makes possible the latter.

Baptism in the Holy Spirit can therefore be seen as the moment when we say a clear and unequivocal yes to the Holy Spirit whom we have already received. In other words, we might describe it as completing our Christian initiation. Our yes releases the power of the Spirit that was always present within us. Finally, we play our part, and in faith we affirm the Christian commitment of our baptism and confirmation. Baptism in the Spirit, therefore, fans into a flame the gift of God already received (2 Timothy 1:6).

The relationship between baptism in the Holy Spirit and the sacraments of Christian initiation is very important. A sacrament is always valid *ex opere operato*—in other words, by the very fact that it is given. But the Church also teaches us that the real fruitfulness of the sacrament in someone's life is *ex opere operantis*. That means it depends on the following subjective factors:

- the quality of the preparation;
- the belief and commitment of the person ministering the sacrament;
- the faith, expectation, and understanding of the person receiving the sacrament.

If there is little faith and low expectation, not much change or fruit will be evident in the recipient's life. Both Scripture and the writings of the Church Fathers clearly show that the normal results of baptism and confirmation were a powerful release of God's love and power, resulting in transformed lives. What then followed was powerful and effective evangelization, accompanied by the use of charismatic gifts.

All this is in direct contrast to what we normally find today. If we want to see a full release of the power of these sacraments, we need to teach and minister baptism in the Holy Spirit. Baptism in the Spirit is never a substitute for the sacraments, but when people ask for a new outpouring of the Spirit and their lives are transformed, they will often refer to baptism in the Spirit as their moment of real conversion, when they personally met Jesus as their living Lord and Savior. It is their personal Pentecost moment.

So although the Spirit was always present, he was hardly noticeable or effective because we were ignorant of the need to surrender to him, or in some cases, we simply decided not to do so. When we do surrender, the Spirit within us is suddenly set free, and the full power in the sacraments of our initiation is released. Then we begin to live committed and courageous Christian lives.

Most of us do not consciously resist the Holy Spirit, as Stephen accused the Sanhedrin of doing (Acts 7:51). But perhaps we need to hear Paul's exhortation in 1 Thessalonians 5:19, "Do not quench the Spirit," which is effectively what we are doing when we ignore the Spirit's presence within us. In this first school of thought, because there has been a total giving of the Spirit when we received the sacraments of Christian initiation, subsequent prayer for baptism in the Spirit simply results in a conscious experience of the release of the power that has already been received. But for a number of reasons, this cannot be all that happens:

- It seems to limit the great prayer *Veni Creator Spiritus*, which is prayed by the Catholic Church on so many occasions, inviting the Spirit to come in a new way.

- It seems to question the traditional belief that there is always a new coming of the Spirit at important moments, both sacramental and simply prayerful ones. For example, when a man is ordained a priest, there is a new sending of the Spirit with gifts to equip him for his new ministry, in just the same way as the Spirit comes with the other sacraments. On September 11, 2010, Pope Benedict XVI spoke to newly consecrated bishops at Castel Gandolfo, Italy, and told them: "In all your duties you are sustained by the Holy Spirit, who, during your Ordination configured you to Christ, the Eternal High Priest."[9]

- Are we also saying that when we pray, "Come, Holy Spirit," we do not really expect a new outpouring of the Spirit because it happened once and for all when we were baptized? Of course not! The Spirit came then and comes again now.

So while it is certain that baptism in the Holy Spirit releases more of the grace received when we were baptized and confirmed, I am certain that there is also always a new sending of the Spirit when we pray, "Come, Holy Spirit!"

A new outpouring
The second school of thought is that it is a new outpouring. Baptism in the Holy Spirit is a powerful new sending of the

Spirit in response to our invitation. The person asking may well have been baptized and confirmed, but sometimes they have not. Jesus pours out his Holy Spirit in amazing new ways in response to our invitation, and while it may be unusual, we can point to occasions in the New Testament when the Spirit is poured out before water baptism has taken place. We can also cite examples today of people who are filled with the Spirit without being baptized in water.

When looking at some Evangelical and most Pentecostal experiences, we see that when a person prays a prayer of repentance and commitment to Christ, they receive the Holy Spirit and may manifest one or more of the gifts of the Spirit, particularly the gift of speaking in tongues. For them, water baptism will often come later. So in this second school of thought, when we ask to be baptized in the Holy Spirit, there is simply a powerful new sending of the Spirit.

In the New Testament, the outpouring of the Spirit always resulted in clear evidence of his presence in the recipients. What occurred when Peter entered the household of Cornelius is often described as the "Pentecost of the Gentiles."

While Peter was still speaking these words, the Holy Spirit came on all who heard the message. The circumcised believers who had come with Peter were astonished that the gift of the Holy Spirit had been poured out even on Gentiles. For they heard them speaking in tongues and praising God. Then Peter said, "Surely no one can stand in the way of their being baptized with water. They have received the Holy Spirit just as we have." So he ordered that they be baptized in the name of Jesus Christ. (Acts 10:44-48)

When Paul writes to the "foolish" Christians in Galatia, his irritation is caused by the fact that he had seen the Spirit freely working in them, but now they have gone back to relying on their own efforts. We must all be on our guard against this temptation:

> After beginning by means of the Spirit, are you now trying to finish by means of the flesh? Have you experienced so much in vain—if it really was in vain? So again I ask, does God give you his Spirit and work miracles among you by the works of the law, or by your believing what you heard? (Galatians 3:3-5)

Change validates experience

These and other New Testament passages indicate that any new sending of the Spirit should result in a noticeable change in the recipients, and the change validates the experience. When in 1976 I experienced the Holy Spirit at work in me in new ways, I realized there had certainly been a new sending or outpouring of the Spirit in response to the prayer that was prayed and my openness to receive him. The Anglican priest who prayed over me told me that he believed God was going to change my life. The dramatic nature of the changes that followed would have been impossible without a new outpouring of the Holy Spirit. Yes, the graces of my baptism and confirmation were fully at work for the first time, but I am certain there was also a new outpouring of the Spirit to equip me for all that lay ahead. This seems to fit well with the views of St. Thomas Aquinas:

> There is an invisible sending also with respect to an advance in virtue or an increase in grace. . . . Such an invisible sending is

especially to be seen in that kind of increase in grace whereby a person moves forward into some new act or some new state of grace: as, for instance, when a person moves forward into the grace of working miracles, or of prophecy.[10]

When we consider this text, it is quite clear that St. Thomas is writing about new sendings of the Spirit to equip people with a special grace for some new activities, and the examples he offers are charismatic rather than sacramental graces. But it is also clear from the writings of St. Thomas that such new sendings are always related to a change in a person's relationship with God, to a significant move forward.

This has been the experience of so many saints and holy men and women who, at profound moments of change or conversion, have received a spontaneous new sending of the Spirit that is not linked to their sacramental baptism. At such moments they have also received special charisms—graces freely given to equip them for new areas of service. This was the experience of Sts. Francis of Assisi, Ignatius of Loyola, Teresa of Avila, and many others.

The key to receiving lies in asking, and in the Letter of James we are reminded that sometimes we do not receive from God because we do not ask: "You do not have because you do not ask God" (4:2). In both schools of thought, inviting the Spirit is the key to receiving.

Can we combine these two schools of thought?
I am at home with both of these schools of thought working together. If, as the first view suggests, we have not availed ourselves of the grace received at our sacramental baptism and

confirmation, we certainly need to consciously do so, thereby releasing the fullness of the restricted grace. But when we pray, "Come, Holy Spirit," we must also be expectant that there will be a new sending of the Spirit, a new outpouring of grace—one that will have immediate and visible effects.

I can live with some lack of clarity in the relationship between the releasing and the sending, or that which has already been given and that which is newly given, since I have often seen God do things that I never expected him to do. So when it comes to the things of the Holy Spirit, I am open to God's surprises.

My simple view is that when we speak of baptism in the Holy Spirit, we are speaking of God working in the lives of individual men and women who come alive in their faith in remarkable new ways. So it seems to me that in this awakening of faith, there is certainly a release of what is already present within us, the power of the Holy Spirit received at baptism, but there is also a new outpouring of the Spirit.

After all, the first disciples experienced a remarkable outpouring of the Spirit in the upper room on Pentecost, but only a short time later, they received another outpouring of the Spirit when they prayed for boldness to preach the word. "After they prayed, the place where they were meeting was shaken. And they were all filled with the Holy Spirit and spoke the word of God boldly" (Acts 4:31). It almost sounds like a second Pentecost, and this was clearly another outpouring of the Spirit in power and with physical signs. We need the Holy Spirit to be poured out on us many times.

In 1 Thessalonians 4:8, Paul writes that God "gives you his Holy Spirit," and for me, this is not just at baptism and confirmation but again and again. However, the gift will not be forced upon me, and if I do not believe in the person and the power of the Holy Spirit and know that God is giving him, I will not ask. Then I will not receive either a new sending of this gift of God or a release of the Spirit already present within me.

Come, Holy Spirit!

Today we pray, "Come, Holy Spirit!" in both formal and informal ways, and this is accepted as perfectly proper and correct. When we pray this prayer, we should expect there to be a new coming of the Holy Spirit to strengthen us for what lies ahead—just as there was when the disciples prayed for a new boldness in Acts 4:31.

So today I am of the opinion there is always a new sending of the Spirit when we pray, "Come, Holy Spirit!" or "Lord, fill me with your Spirit!" or "Lord, baptize me in your Holy Spirit!" But the first time we consciously do this, the grace already given at our baptism and confirmation is also released within us, resulting in an explosion of Holy Spirit power in our lives. This is what we call baptism in the Spirit. The pragmatic side of me simply says, "Don't worry too much about the explanations; just ask. God will answer, and you will know the presence and power of the Holy Spirit in your life—you can deal with the explanations later." This is how theology is supposed to work anyway.

The result can be a sudden and dramatic change accompanied by overwhelming emotions: joy, praise, repentance, tears, or love. Or we can experience almost nothing and only realize that something has happened when we look back at what has changed over a period of weeks or months.

So I am sure that for those already baptized, there is both a release and a new sending of the Spirit when we ask Jesus to baptize us in his Holy Spirit. I am delighted that some fine theologians are presenting good arguments for the work of the Holy Spirit; this is essential. But sadly, their papers will rarely reach the person in the pew. For most of us, baptism in the Spirit is a grace that can only be understood by looking for changes in the lives of those who say they have received it. Let's avoid the temptation to concentrate on the how and what of baptism in the Holy Spirit and just accept that the prayer of invitation is effective: we ask, he comes. But unless we know that there is a Holy Spirit who wants to come to us, and unless we believe in him and know that he will be given, we will never ask, and we will never experience his coming.

A moment of surrender

There has to be a moment of surrender, a moment when we say an unreserved yes to God in a deep and powerful way:

- yes to who he is and all that he has done for us;
- yes to all that he wants to give us;
- yes and welcome to the life-changing, indwelling Holy Spirit;
- yes to his will and no to our own selfish desires.

This is baptism in the Holy Spirit, freely available to all who are willing to step out and say this yes. Through it, a full life of faith is no longer just a possibility; it can become a reality. But for many, this amazing gift of the Spirit has been received but never opened. We need to open the gift.

2. How do we describe baptism in the Holy Spirit?

It is the fulfillment of the promise of the Father: "How much more will your Father in heaven give the Holy Spirit to those who ask him!" (Luke 11:13).

It is the fulfillment of the promise of the Son: "Unless I go away, the Advocate will not come to you; but if I go, I will send him to you" (John 16:7).

It results in a closer, transformed relationship with Jesus as Lord: "No one can say, 'Jesus is Lord,' except by the Holy Spirit" (1 Corinthians 12:3).

It introduces us to God as a loving Father: "The Spirit you received brought about your adoption to sonship. And by him we cry, 'Abba, Father'"* (Romans 8:15).

It is an experience that makes both Jesus and the Father real to us: "We proclaim to you what we have seen and heard, so that you also may have fellowship with us. And our fellowship is with the Father and with his Son, Jesus Christ" (1 John 1:3).

It results in spontaneous vocal praise and worship of God: "We hear them declaring the wonders of God in our own tongues!" (Acts 2:11).

It makes us more aware of the importance of sacramental baptism as our new birth in Christ: "No one can enter the kingdom of God unless they are born of water and the Spirit" (John 3:5).

It is the provision of power and zeal to serve and to evangelize: "You will receive power when the Holy Spirit comes on you; and you will be my witnesses" (Acts 1:8). Blessed Pope Paul VI wrote, "Evangelization will never be possible without the action of the Holy Spirit."[11]

It is the entrance into the spiritual gifts for mission and service: "Now to each one the manifestation of the Spirit is given for the common good" (1 Corinthians 12:7; see *Lumen Gentium,* 12).

It promotes a greater awareness of the importance of social justice: "The Spirit of the Lord is on me, / because he has anointed me / to proclaim good news to the poor. / He has sent me to proclaim freedom for the prisoners / and recovery of sight for the blind, / to set the oppressed free" (Luke 4:18).

It makes us aware of the spiritual battle between the forces of light and darkness: "For our struggle is . . . against the powers of this dark world and against the spiritual forces of evil in the heavenly realms" (Ephesians 6:12).

It is often a physical experience: "After they prayed, the place where they were meeting was shaken. And they were all filled with the Holy Spirit" (Acts 4:31).

It creates that greater unity among Christians for which Jesus prayed: "That they may be brought to complete unity . . . [so that] the world will know that you sent me" (John 17:23).

It allows the Spirit to work in us to produce more fruit: "The fruit of the Spirit is love, joy, peace, forbearance, kindness . . . " (Galatians 5:22-26).

It is not a once-and-for-all experience—we must go on being filled with the Holy Spirit: "Be filled with the Spirit" (Ephesians 5:18).

It is freely given: "How much more will your Father in heaven give the Holy Spirit to those who ask him!" (Luke 11:13).

Forgive me for repeating: baptism in the Holy Spirit is not something we earn or merit, and none of the results come about through our own ability. It is a gift from God, freely given to those who ask. It is the presence, love, life, and power of God, freely given to us to renew us both inwardly and outwardly and to enable us to live a full and effective Christian life. When we ask to be baptized in the Holy Spirit, it is Jesus the baptizer we are seeking—he is the One who baptizes us in his Spirit. When he does so, his Holy Spirit does not just provide the supernatural power we need to live our Christian life, but equally important, he comes to us as a loving friend and helper to protect and guide us in everything we do. Let us always remember that Jesus and his Spirit are never apart— they are "conjoined and inseparable"(*Catechism,* 743).

Baptism in the Spirit is at the same time a release of the restricted graces of our baptism and confirmation and a new outpouring of the grace and power of the Holy Spirit. It is available to us at any time in our lives and supplies what has been missing as a result of an inadequate response to our Christian initiation. In a certain way, it shows the institutional (sacraments) and charismatic (gifts) dimensions in the life of the Church working together to produce a powerful and effective result—committed disciples on fire with the Spirit.

To baptize means "to plunge into" or "to immerse in." When we are initiated as Christians and baptized in water, we are plunged into Christ and into his body, the Church. We are washed of original sin, the first step in our salvation, and because we receive Christ, we also receive his Spirit. Baptism in the Spirit is when Jesus, as he promised, plunges us into his Holy Spirit. He is the baptizer, and the Holy Spirit is the One into whom we are plunged. All this is to help us be effective Christians, to equip us to serve. It happens because we ask for it, and we are plunged into the life of God himself.

The promise

God's promise that we will be baptized in the Holy Spirit occurs in the New Testament, once in each Gospel and then in the Book of Acts:

- "He [Jesus] will baptize you with the Holy Spirit and fire" (Matthew 3:11).
- "He [Jesus] will baptize you with the Holy Spirit" (Mark 1:8).

- "He [Jesus] will baptize you with the Holy Spirit and fire" (Luke 3:16).
- "[Jesus] . . . is the one who will baptize with the Holy Spirit" (John 1:33).
- "In a few days you will be baptized with the Holy Spirit" (Acts 1:5).

As the early church community began to spread the gospel, we find a number of accounts of new Christians receiving the Holy Spirit, including these:

- Peter on Pentecost: "You will receive the gift of the Holy Spirit" (see Acts 2:38-39).
- Peter and John in Samaria: "They received the Holy Spirit" (see Acts 8:14-17).
- Peter with Cornelius: "The Holy Spirit came on all" (see Acts 10:44-46).
- Paul in Ephesus: "When Paul placed his hands on them, the Holy Spirit came on them, and they spoke in tongues and prophesied" (see Acts 19:1-6).

In the Book of Acts, we find that the word "filled" is frequently used:

- On Pentecost: "All of them were filled with the Holy Spirit" (Acts 2:4).
- Peter before the Sanhedrin: "Then Peter, filled with the Holy Spirit, said to them . . . " (Acts 4:8).
- At the choosing of the seven deacons: "Choose seven men . . . who are known to be full of the Spirit and wisdom.

... They chose Stephen, a man full of faith and of the Holy Spirit" (Acts 6:3, 5).

"Baptized in the Holy Spirit" and "filled with the Holy Spirit" are the normal phrases found in the Bible. Some other terms used today instead of "baptism in the Spirit" are "renewed in the Spirit," "released in the Spirit," "anointed with the Spirit," and "immersed in the Spirit." It can also be referred to as "the outpouring of the Spirit" or "the rekindling of the Spirit."

But the description is not really important, nor is the way in which it happens. We are all individuals, and God deals with us uniquely and personally. What is important is that we receive the fullness of the Spirit—his love, life, and power—making us effective Christians, with God now free to work in and through us.

It was estimated that over 120 million Catholics had been baptized in the Holy Spirit by 2001.[12] By 2017, the fiftieth anniversary of the Catholic Charismatic Renewal, it is estimated that this number could be 200 million. When we add the number from the mainline Protestant churches and include the Pentecostal and charismatic independent or nondenominational churches, we find that one-third of global Christians will say they have experienced this amazing outpouring of grace and have been filled with the Holy Spirit.

If we look deeper, we will discover that this one-third is the fastest growing part of the Christian church worldwide and, at the current rate, could represent half of all Christians by 2025. We should be on our knees in thanksgiving, because whatever our spirituality or denomination, we need to take baptism in the Holy Spirit very seriously indeed. It is not something just for a group of enthusiasts—it's vitally important for all of us if we are to receive the fullness of the Father's gift to his children, and it is offered to everyone who asks for it. Against this background and with all this in mind, we'll move on to our next question.

3. How can we receive this new life in the Holy Spirit?

We have already looked at this question in chapter 2, and we have seen that new life in the Spirit is a gift, but we need to ask for it. Jesus said,

> "Let anyone who is thirsty come to me and drink. Whoever believes in me, as Scripture has said, rivers of living water will flow from within them." By this he meant the Spirit, whom those who believed in him were later to receive. Up to that time the Spirit had not been given, since Jesus had not yet been glorified. (John 7:37-39)

Living water is always flowing, bringing life to desert places as the prophets tell us, "For I will pour water on the thirsty land, / and streams on the dry ground; / I will pour out my Spirit on your offspring, / and my blessing on your descendants" (Isaiah 44:3). And as Jesus explains to the Samaritan woman at Jacob's well, "Whoever drinks the water I give them will never thirst. Indeed, the water I give them will become in them a spring of living water welling up to eternal life" (John 4:14).

So we must acknowledge our need, we must want to receive this new life, and then we must come to Jesus and ask for it.

We need to believe in him and in the promise, and we may need to deal with doubts, fears, barriers, and obstacles that stand in the way. It will certainly be important to repent of our sins and to want to be right with God (Acts 2:38-39). But this does not mean that we have to be perfect, because if we did, we would be waiting forever! When the Spirit comes in power, he will convict us of sin (John 16:8). Repentance will usually be the doorway to receiving the fullness of the Spirit, but sometimes it comes after being filled with the Holy Spirit, because until then we may not be able to see the areas in our lives where we need to change.

Many just don't see the need to repent, and this can be the biggest obstacle between God and us, but the Spirit will show us our sin. God deals with us step by step. If he revealed to us all that needed to change in one moment, we might give up before we even begin. The Christian life is a journey of discovery.

Let me repeat those key words: *need, want, come, ask, repent, receive.*

Jesus can baptize us in his Holy Spirit at any time and in any place. We may be alone or in a crowd; often we will be with others who have already received this new life, and they will lay hands on us and pray with us (Acts 8:17; 19:5-6). We may have decided that we need to open our lives to the Holy Spirit and so have followed a course of teaching similar to this one, or we may spontaneously choose to ask Jesus to baptize us in the Spirit without any formal teaching. God is sovereign and deals with us as individuals; no two people have the same experience of the Spirit at work in them. "How" and "when" are not the most important issues—what matters is that we are filled with the Spirit.

4. Are there any hindrances to receiving this new life in the Holy Spirit?

Yes, there are, and I will very briefly highlight some of them:

Sin: We need to repent of any major sin in our lives of which we are aware. We should be clean vessels for the Lord to fill with his Spirit. Often we don't see the need for repentance, but God will show us if we ask. It may happen that we only become aware of some areas of sin after we have been filled with the Spirit.

Ignorance: Some may think that baptism in the Spirit is a shortcut to holiness. This is not the case, but because we have the Holy Spirit alive in us in a new way, he will help us enter into the holiness that is God's gift to us. Nor is baptism in the Spirit a spiritual status symbol denoting a super-Christian. In fact, it reveals how much work remains to be done in us. Baptism in the Spirit may wrongly be seen as a goal, whereas it is just a new beginning in our exciting journey of faith—there's always more. It may be regarded as something to solve all our problems, whereas in fact it will highlight them. But the good news is that the Spirit will now equip us to address them. It takes courage to face the truth about ourselves.

Wrong motives: Some may seek baptism in the Spirit for their own reasons. We must accept God's priorities. These have as their focus witness, evangelization, service, and ministry to others. The Spirit is not given to show how wonderful you and I are, but to show everyone how great Jesus is.

Fear: We may be afraid of what will happen to us, what God will ask of us, or where he will take us. So we need to remember that this is a gift from God to his children. It will help us and be good for us. But it takes courage to change; staying as we are usually feels more comfortable. Or we may be afraid of what others will think or say. We need to trust God and not allow human respect to control us. It takes courage to stand for our new convictions when we know they'll be challenged.

Pride: I have often heard remarks like, "Why do I need this? I've been a good Catholic all my life." We may genuinely think we have all we need; but this is a form of pride, and it makes us unteachable. Often we feel a need to be in control; this is pride, and it needs to be surrendered. Or we may be proud of our secular mind-set and unwilling to surrender it.

Resentment: There may be things that have happened in our lives that have caused major resentment to build up in us toward a person or a group of people. Perhaps we feel we have been wronged, and there may even be some justification for this view, but our unwillingness to forgive will block the work of the Holy Spirit in us. Forgiving someone is a decision we make even when we don't "feel" like forgiving that person. By surrendering our resentment, we are released to receive more of the Holy Spirit.

Works: Many of us still think we have to somehow earn or deserve God's favor to be worthy of it. But this discounts God's grace, his desire to freely give us something we cannot deserve or earn. All we must do is believe, come, and ask.

Unworthiness: Yes, we are unworthy, but amazingly, to God we are of enormous value: sinners for whom he gave his only Son, lost sheep for whom he searches. Jesus made us worthy.

Unbelief: A vague hope dishonors God. We need to confess our lack of faith and put our full trust in Jesus. This takes courage. Here is how Pope Benedict defined faith: "Faith is first and foremost a personal, intimate encounter with Jesus; it is having an experience of his closeness, his friendship, and his love. It is in this way that we learn to know him ever better, to love him and to follow him more and more. May this happen to each one of us."[13]

5. What is likely to happen after we have received this gift from God?

Because God deals with everyone as an individual, no one can give a universal answer. But some positive things are likely to happen, and some traps must be avoided.

Prayer: When someone experiences a new outpouring of the Holy Spirit, it's certain that they will want to pray more and will discover that the Spirit helps them to pray. "We do not know what we ought to pray for, but the Spirit himself intercedes for us" (Romans 8:26).

Scripture: There will be a new interest in the Bible, a desire to read it, and a better understanding of what is read. Scripture will come alive in a new way. This is often accompanied by a willingness to be subject to God's word: "All Scripture is

God–breathed and is useful for teaching, rebuking, correcting, and training in righteousness, so that the servant of God may be thoroughly equipped for every good work" (2 Timothy 3:16-17). St. John Paul II wrote, "May the Holy Bible continue to be a treasure for the Church and for every Christian. . . . Let us take up this book! Let us receive it from the Lord who continually offers it to us through his Church (cf. Revelation 10:8). Let us devour it (cf. 10:9), so that it can become our very life. . . . Filled with hope, we will be able to share it with every man and woman whom we encounter on our way."[14]

Sacraments: The sacraments will become more important, especially the Eucharist and the Sacrament of Reconciliation. "For whenever you eat this bread and drink this cup, you proclaim the Lord's death until he comes" (1 Corinthians 11:26). "We implore you on Christ's behalf: Be reconciled to God" (2 Corinthians 5:20). As Pope St. John Paul II wrote, "A prominent place needs to be given to the celebration of the sacraments, . . . in the knowledge that in them Christ himself is acting through the Holy Spirit."[15]

Personal holiness: Once someone has experienced baptism in the Spirit, he will often have a new desire to live a holy life in the power of the Spirit. "But now that you have been set free from sin and have become slaves of God, the benefit you reap leads to holiness, and the result is eternal life" (Romans 6:22).

Joy, praise, and worship: When the Spirit is alive in us, it is entirely natural that we will have a greater joy and desire to thank, praise, and worship God, both publicly and privately.

"Is anyone happy? Let them sing songs of praise" (James 5:13). Pope Francis told a large gathering of charismatics in Rome, "When I would celebrate Mass in the cathedral in Buenos Aires with the charismatic renewal, after the consecration and a few moments of adoration in tongues, we would sing this hymn ["Jesus the Lord Lives"] with great joy and fervor, as you have today. Thank you! I felt at home!"[16]

A desire for the Second Coming: A new interest in Christ's Second Coming is often aroused: "For while we are in this tent, we groan and are burdened, because we do not wish to be unclothed but to be clothed instead with our heavenly dwelling, so that what is mortal may be swallowed up by life. Now the one who has fashioned us for this very purpose is God, who has given us the Spirit as a deposit, guaranteeing what is to come" (2 Corinthians 5:4-5).

Love for God and our neighbor and a desire for community: The first result of a new release of the Holy Spirit will always be an increase in love. We will be filled with the love of God the Father and of his Son, Jesus Christ. Our hearts of stone are broken and replaced with hearts of flesh (Ezekiel 36:26), and this experience of God's love will affect all our relationships. Most people find that they have a new love for people they were not previously drawn to. This leads to a desire to be more involved in the local church or community and to seek fellowship with those who share the same experience of the Spirit. There will also be a new desire for justice and a willingness to help those in trouble. The Book of Acts encapsulates what resulted when the Spirit came in power:

They devoted themselves to the apostles' teaching and to fellowship, to the breaking of bread and to prayer. Everyone was filled with awe at the many wonders and signs performed by the apostles. All the believers were together and had everything in common. They sold property and possessions to give to anyone who had need. Every day they continued to meet together in the temple courts. They broke bread in their homes and ate together with glad and sincere hearts, praising God and enjoying the favor of all the people. And the Lord added to their number daily those who were being saved. (Acts 2:42-47)

There is no reason why we should not expect very similar results when the Holy Spirit is free to work in us. Wouldn't it be wonderful if that Scripture passage from Acts describing the life of the early Christians also described life in our parishes today? But the greatest and the most essential result of baptism in the Holy Spirit, the one that is most life-changing, is the realization that Jesus is Lord: "No one can say, 'Jesus is Lord,' except by the Holy Spirit" (I Corinthians 12:3).

However, there are some pitfalls to be avoided:

Pride—again! No one person is better than another, but God is gracious to all who seek him and ask. To avoid the dangers of spiritual pride, it is helpful to take on new areas of service in the church or to carry out the more difficult and unpopular tasks. "I hate pride and arrogance" (Proverbs 8:13).

Criticism: There is a danger of feeling superior to those who have not received a new outpouring of the Spirit. This may result in criticizing what we see as their limited vision and expectation of God. God does not want this. "For in the same way you judge others, you will be judged" (Matthew 7:2).

Cooling off: We cannot expect to stay at the top of the mountain, but we must be careful not to lose our enthusiasm. We need to stay close to the Lord: "I am the vine; you are the branches" (John 15:5).

Seeking extraordinary experiences: Some people go from place to place in search of the latest experience or novelty. St. Paul describes this: "They will gather around them a great number of teachers to say what their itching ears want to hear" (2 Timothy 4:3). The challenge is to get involved in normal, everyday life, bringing Christ more and more into our homes, our places of work and leisure, and our parishes.

When we experience new life in the Spirit, we may spend time in the desert, just like Jesus did: "Jesus . . . was led by the Spirit into the wilderness" (Luke 4:1). This is to test us, and it will make us stronger in our faith. Temptations will come, but we are equipped to deal with them, and they should not discourage us. But while we are in a new place spiritually, it's only the beginning. We need to learn how to walk in the love and power of God's Holy Spirit. As Paul told the Galatian Christians: "Since we live by the Spirit, let us keep in step with the Spirit. Let us not become conceited, provoking and envying each other" (5:25-26).

Come and claim the promise!

To sum up: baptism in the Holy Spirit is the fulfillment of the promise of the Father, released to us by the work of Jesus. It is a free gift, given to those who are thirsty and who ask. So we must come thirsty, repentant, obedient, and full of faith—to claim the promise requires a definite act of faith. We may face all sorts of doubts and questions. What will happen? Will it work? What will others think? Will I have to change?

Or perhaps we think it seems too easy, too good to be true. But God has promised, so we come to claim his promise and to receive his gift of new life in the Spirit. He will not disappoint us! It's good to keep in mind that the most important evidence of baptism in the Holy Spirit is not the presence of miraculous signs but, rather, the new revelation of the person of Jesus Christ. We see him in a new way, and our response is "Yes, Lord!" Something in us changes. Stanley Jebb, a Baptist minister, once expressed it like this:

> The baptism in the Spirit provides power in witness, a new ability in prayer, an entrance into the realm of spiritual gifts, and a willingness to suffer for Christ. None of these things come through our own ability. All depend on the enabling grace of God through his Holy Spirit. One of the loveliest results of this experience is a deeper love for the Lord and for one another, and the coming of the Holy Spirit results in greater unity among believers.[17]

On Pentecost Sunday, May 11, 2008, Pope Benedict XVI publicly challenged us to rediscover what it means to be baptized in the Holy Spirit:

Jesus' entire mission aimed at giving the Spirit of God to men and women and at baptizing them in his regenerative "bath." This was brought about with his glorification (cf. John 7:39), that is, through his death and resurrection: then the Spirit of God was poured out in superabundance, like a cascade capable of purifying every heart, extinguishing the fire of evil, and kindling the flame of divine love in the world. . . . Today I would like to extend the invitation to all: let us rediscover, dear brothers and sisters, the beauty of being baptized in the Holy Spirit; let us recover awareness of our Baptism and our Confirmation, ever timely sources of grace.[18]

Earlier, in a homily on the feast of the Baptism of the Lord on January 13, 2008, Pope Benedict had spoken these words: "Jesus was revealed as the One who came to baptize humanity in the Holy Spirit: he came to give men and women life in abundance" (cf. John 10:10).[19]

These statements by Pope Benedict help us to understand the link between our sacramental baptism and baptism in the Holy Spirit. We are expected to experience the Spirit in a superabundant way, like a waterfall purifying our hearts, destroying evil, and igniting the fire of God's love. Baptism in the Spirit occurs when we open our lives to this powerful waterfall of the Holy Spirit, which brings us life to the full (John 10:10).

With all this on offer, who can possibly hold back?

6. How can we pray for someone to be baptized in the Holy Spirit?

There is not really a right or wrong way to pray with someone for baptism in the Holy Spirit—God is sovereign and will act as he chooses (we know this from Acts 10:44-48). However, there are some factors to consider.

Anyone may receive prayer for baptism in the Holy Spirit at any time and in any place, but it is likely to be more effective when a person is seeking it for the right reasons (see pages 71–73) and has understood that he or she should prepare for it spiritually. One of the most common ways to approach baptism in the Holy Spirit is by following a course of six or seven sessions, usually described as a Life in the Spirit Seminar. This course clearly presents the basic Christian teaching and is often offered by parishes, communities, prayer groups, or similar groups. It includes talks, sharing, and discussion in small groups, and gives ample opportunity for personal questions and clarifications. This book can also be used as the basis for a Life in the Spirit Seminar.

The actual prayer for baptism in the Holy Spirit will often be offered by the leaders of the seminars and small groups. It consists of an invitation to Jesus to pour out his Holy Spirit upon the person and into his or her life in a new way, and to release the power of the Spirit already present in the person if they have been baptized. The prayer will normally be accompanied by the laying on of hands (Acts 8:17) and an expectation that with this new outpouring of the Spirit will come one or more of the supernatural gifts listed in 1 Corinthians 12 and dealt with in chapters 4 and 5 of this book. These are gifts, not rights; they require an openness on the part of the person being prayed with, and will be given according to God's will and not the person's choice. The results to be expected after the prayer are discussed in the coming chapters.

I encourage every reader to request prayer for this blessing of baptism in the Holy Spirit, confident that the Lord will respond to our invitation: *"Come, Holy Spirit!"*

Questions for Reflection and Discussion

1. Being baptized in the Holy Spirit is the fulfillment of the promise of the Father through Jesus, and it is his gift to every Christian who asks for it. What would you say to someone who asks for an explanation of this gift?

2. We can all receive this gift and enter fully into the new life in the Spirit. Why, then, do you think so many people do not ask for the gift?

3. There may be hindrances and objections to be dealt with. What are they, and are you aware of any of them being present in your life?

4. In what ways are there links between the Sacraments of Baptism and Confirmation and baptism in the Holy Spirit? If you have already received the Holy Spirit when you were baptized, why do you need prayer for baptism in the Holy Spirit?

5. What are some of the pitfalls to be avoided after receiving baptism in the Holy Spirit?

Helpful Scripture passages to pray:
    Luke 3:16
    Acts 2:1-4
    Galatians 3:3-5
    John 7:37
    John 10:10

Chapter Four

The Gifts of the Holy Spirit

1. What are the spiritual gifts or charisms, and to whom are they given?
2. Which particular gifts of the Holy Spirit are we talking about?

Where does this word "charism" come from, and what exactly does it mean? The root is found in the Greek word *charis,* meaning "grace," and *charisma,* meaning "a work of grace" or "a gift of grace." Every charism is a special gift of grace because it is given supernaturally by an intervention of the Holy Spirit to equip a person to undertake a particular task or service for the benefit of the Church. In the view of St. Paul, the charisms show the particular function we have in the Christian community, where there will be a rich variety of charisms in operation. This teaching of St. Paul is fully endorsed in *Lumen Gentium,* the Second Vatican Council's important document on the nature of the Church, as we will see.

Charisms are not for our personal sanctification but are given for the benefit of the community. "Each of you should use whatever gift you have received to serve others, as faithful stewards of God's grace in its various forms" (1 Peter 4:10). Paul reaffirms this idea, saying, "We have different gifts, according to the grace given to each of us. If your gift is prophesying, then prophesy . . . ; if it is serving, then serve; if it is teaching, then teach" (Romans 12:6-7).

When we search the Scriptures, we find examples of many gifts and ministries given by the Holy Spirit, but for the purposes of our study, I will be concentrating on the list of charisms or special graces referred to by St. Paul in chapter 12 of his first letter to the Corinthians. Here he was not giving an introduction to the charisms—he was clearly writing to a community that was already familiar with the charisms but was misusing these gifts of the Holy Spirit.

So in order to fully appreciate his teaching, we really need to study chapters 13 and 14 as well, since these chapters deal with the climate in which the gifts are to be used and emphasize the importance of always making sure there is good order. For our purposes, however, we first need to examine his list of gifts in chapter 12 in some detail, consider why we need them in today's advanced and sophisticated world, and then take a more general look at how we are to use them.

Dealing with ignorance

"Now about the gifts of the Spirit, brothers and sisters, I do not want you to be uninformed" (1 Corinthians 12:1). Paul's opening sentence makes it clear that when it came to the spiritual gifts or charisms, there was ignorance in this early Christian community.

Things have not changed much—there is still a lot of ignorance today, and many people know nothing about the spiritual gifts, not even that they exist. The difference, however, is that in the church of Corinth there was an excessive use of some of the gifts, causing disorder in their meetings, whereas today there is a lack of use of the gifts in our churches. We are missing something important.

Today some believe the charismatic gifts were given to the early church but have since been withdrawn (a cessationist view), while others think they are now only given in exceptional circumstances to very holy and specially chosen people—the saints. Neither of these views is correct, nor is the view that came into the Church during the Age of Enlightenment, when many were skeptical of the supernatural and believed that everything could be explained by reason. None of these views conform to Scripture and the teaching of the Church today (see *Catechism*, 798–801).

The topic of spiritual gifts was debated at the second session of the Second Vatican Council in October 1963. It centered on whether in our day the charisms are given to many of the faithful so that they can help to build up the Church or whether such gifts are extremely rare and exceptional. The view that prevailed was that it is not only through the sacraments and official ministries that the Holy Spirit equips and leads the Church, but that the charisms are special graces, which are also essential for the life of the Church. The Holy Spirit still distributes them among the faithful of every rank, and they are to be received with gratitude and used for the renewal and building up of the Church.

As a result of the debate about the charisms, we find this teaching in the document *Lumen Gentium* from the Fathers of Vatican II:

It is not only through the sacraments and the ministries of the Church that the Holy Spirit sanctifies and leads the people of God and enriches it with virtues, but, "allotting his gifts to everyone according as he wills" (1 Corinthians 12:11), he distributes special graces among the faithful of every rank. By these gifts He makes them fit and ready to undertake the various tasks and offices which contribute toward the renewal and building up of the Church. . . . These charisms, whether they be the more outstanding or the more simple and widely diffused, are to be received with thanksgiving and consolation for they are perfectly suited to and useful for the needs of the Church.[20]

This teaching is very clearly based on the teaching of St. Paul, particularly in 1 Corinthians 12, which we will be examining in more detail.

At a special meeting with ecclesial movements and new communities on the eve of Pentecost on May 30, 1998, outside St. Peter's Basilica in Rome, Pope St. John Paul II said this:

Whenever the Spirit intervenes, he leaves people astonished. He brings about events of amazing newness; he radically changes persons and history. This was the unforgettable experience of the Second Vatican Ecumenical Council during which, under the guidance of the same Spirit, the Church rediscovered the charismatic dimension as one of her constitutive elements. . . .

The institutional and charismatic aspects are coessential, as it were, to the Church's constitution. They contribute, although differently, to the life, renewal, and sanctification of God's People. It is from this providential rediscovery of the Church's charismatic dimension that, before and after the Council, a remarkable pattern of growth has been established for ecclesial movements and new communities.[21]

In the *Catechism of the Catholic Church*, we find that

charisms are to be accepted with gratitude by the person who receives them and by all members of the Church as well. They are a wonderfully rich grace for the apostolic vitality and for the holiness of the entire Body of Christ, provided they are really are genuine gifts of the Holy Spirit and are used in full conformity with authentic promptings of this same Spirit, that is, in keeping with charity, the true measure of all charisms. (800)

In a later section, we are told that "whatever their character—sometimes it is extraordinary, such as the gift of miracles or of tongues—charisms are oriented toward sanctifying grace and are intended for the common good of the Church. They are at the service of charity which builds up the Church" (2003).

If this is the case, some might ask, "Why do we need doctrine and teaching when we have the Spirit and his gifts?" To explain this, we can use the analogy of a sailing boat (which I believe originated with Donald Gee, a well-known Pentecostal leader). In addition to its sail, a boat needs quite a heavy keel to give it balance. Without the sail, it will go nowhere, but without the keel, the boat is unbalanced and will tip over. We need the wind of the Spirit to fill our sails and move us forward, but we also need the heavy keel to keep us upright. There is no conflict between doctrine and Spirit, teaching and experience, institutional and charismatic—just a healthy balance. Both are necessary.

Pope St. John Paul II reminded us that the institutional and charismatic dimensions of the Church are both essential to her life. The institutional and structural dimension has been passed down from generation to generation since the time of the apostles, whereas the charismatic dimension bursts into the life of the Church in unexpected ways. The institution needs the charismatic dimension to bring the life of the Spirit into the structures and to the people, as well as to give vision, while the charismatic dimension needs the institution to discern and guide it, protect it, and ensure it is accepted and nurtured. It also needs the discernment of Church authorities to protect it from error.

It has always been the case that the office of apostle is in the first place among the ministries and gifts, and that authority in the Church is therefore vested in the apostles and their successors, the bishops. In Acts 15, Paul and Barnabas report the miraculous signs and wonders they have seen among the Gentiles to the Council of Jerusalem, fully prepared to accept the decision of James and the council members on the question of circumcision of the Gentile converts. In the same way today, those Catholics who have experienced baptism in the Spirit fully accept the authority of the pope and the hierarchy and look to them for discernment, guidance, and support in all matters concerning life in the Spirit and the charismatic gifts.

The attitudes and understanding of Popes Paul VI, John Paul II, Benedict XVI, and Francis have played a vital role in ensuring that the Church has accepted the new movements and communities, encouraging them to take their place in the life of the Church. The popes have understood that the charismatic gifts are not given for personal benefit, nor are they "spiritual trophies" to show how special the recipients are. They are given to equip, enable, and empower the Church as it reaches out to serve the needy world around it and to bring the gospel to everyone. The charisms show God in action, and they will be given to us when we find ourselves in situations in which they are needed. Against this background, let's look at our questions on the charismatic gifts.

1. What are the spiritual gifts or charisms, and to whom are they given?

The spiritual gifts are different supernatural gifts of grace given to us by the Holy Spirit to enrich the lives of those around us: "There are different kinds of gifts, but the same Spirit distributes them. There are different kinds of service, but the same Lord. There are different kinds of working, but in all of them and in everyone it is the same God at work" (1 Corinthians 12:4-6). They are distinct from the gifts listed in Isaiah 11:2: wisdom, understanding, counsel, power, knowledge, and fear of the Lord. When I was confirmed, I was taught that I would receive these gifts of the Spirit for my personal growth and that they would be given to everyone who received a new outpouring of the Holy Spirit in the Sacrament of Confirmation. While these are not the charismatic gifts of grace we are discussing in this chapter, they are still valid and genuine gifts of the Spirit given for a different purpose (*Catechism*, 1831). The weakness of the catechesis at my confirmation was that these were the only gifts I heard about.

It's important to note that *every charism is a gift—but not every gift is a charism.* As we have already seen, the word "charism" means "a special gift of grace" (See *Catechism*, 799). A charism is special because it has a supernatural dimension to it, so it is not the same as a natural talent—which is also a gift from God—but it may add a new dimension to a natural ability. The charisms are the various ways in which special gifts of grace are evident in the lives of individual men and women, making them powerful channels of grace to others in the Christian community and beyond. A charism is a special gift because it is freely given to us, but it belongs to God and not to us. In a certain sense, he "lends" a gift to us for a specific occasion and purpose. Our task is to receive it and use it as the Spirit leads us: "Now to each one the manifestation of the Spirit is given for the common good" (1 Corinthians 12:7).

There is, therefore, no reason for us to be ignorant or afraid. We need to embrace the teaching of Scripture, clearly interpreted by the Church, and be open to the gifts of the Holy Spirit in our own lives, ready to receive them and use them. We are all members of the one body (1 Corinthians 12:12-31), and we are to use the gifts the Spirit gives us. If we do not, others are impoverished, because these gifts are not for our personal benefit but for the good and benefit of those around us. If we are open, God will use us as channels for his gifts so that his life-changing power can reach others.

In the teaching of Paul, the body of Christ is extremely important. It is the visible Church, a community made up of a variety of people with a variety of functions and gifts. It's important to remember that these are gifts, freely given to us according to the sovereign will and purpose of God. They are not prizes or rewards given for particular merit, so they are not something earned or deserved by special people. God is showing us that he is a loving Father who wants to give good gifts that will meet the needs of all his children through ordinary faithful members of his body, not only through ordained ministers. The gifts are

- Spiritual (*pneumatika*)—not talents but special gifts of the Holy Spirit.
- Gifts (*charismata*)—not prizes but freely given as God chooses.
- Services (*diakoniai*)—to serve others, not ourselves.
- Powers (*energemata*)—momentary powers, not permanent possessions.
- Manifestations (*phanerosa*)—visible acts, showing God's presence.

We can summarize these points by saying that the gifts are spiritual powers above our natural abilities, freely given to us by the Holy Spirit, to be used for the benefit of others, and producing definite, often visible, results. All of us are encouraged to "eagerly desire gifts of the Spirit" (1 Corinthians 14:1), but then we must leave it to the Holy Spirit to give them to those he wishes, knowing that he gives us different gifts, "and he distributes them to each one, just as he determines" (12:11). We may desire a particular gift and ask God for it, but it may not be the one he wants to give us. It is his decision, and we must accept his will.

2. Which particular gifts of the Holy Spirit are we talking about?

We believe that we are created by God and that he is the source of all that we have and are. So every good gift comes from him, and this includes our natural abilities and talents as well as the special gifts of grace or charisms he may give us through the Holy Spirit. But here we are still talking about charisms, not natural abilities. We find a number of gifts and ministries in the writings of St. Paul:

> The gifts he gave were that some would be apostles, some prophets, some evangelists, some pastors and teachers, to equip the saints for the work of ministry, for building up the body of Christ. (Ephesians 4:11-12, NRSV)

> We have different gifts, according to the grace given to each of us. If your gift is prophesying, then prophesy in accordance with your faith; if it is serving, then serve; if it is teaching, then teach; if it is to encourage, then give encouragement; if it is giving, then give generously; if it is to lead, do it diligently; if it is to show mercy, do it cheerfully. (Romans 12:6-8)

All these gifts are important for building up the body of Christ, but in these two Scripture passages, Paul is mainly writing about gifts that supernaturally equip people for their particular vocations or callings. Those called to be apostles, prophets, teachers, evangelists, and leaders will fulfill important ministries that will profoundly affect the way they live their lives. Encouraging, giving generously, showing mercy: these are gifts that are more widely distributed in the body. When it comes to the main offices in the Church, charisms both demonstrate the particular function each person has and equip the person to perform that function.

The most discussed list of charisms is found in St. Paul's first letter to the Corinthians, in which he makes it absolutely clear that the gifts of the Spirit are given for the good of everyone and then lists the particular gifts he has in mind:

> Now to each one the manifestation of the Spirit is given for the common good. To one there is given through the Spirit a message of wisdom, to another a message of knowledge by means of the same Spirit, to another faith by the same Spirit, to another gifts of healing by that one Spirit, to another miraculous powers, to another prophecy, to another distinguishing between spirits, to another speaking in different kinds of tongues, and to still another the interpretation of tongues. All these are the work of one and the same Spirit, and he distributes them to each one, just as he determines. (1 Corinthians 12:7-11)

One way to consider these gifts is to divide them into three groups. The divisions are rather artificial, and gifts from different groups are sometimes used together, but I find it a helpful way of approaching them. Group One contains what may be called the "knowing" or "revelation" gifts: the message of wisdom, the message of knowledge, and the distinguishing between spirits. Group Two is made up of the "doing" or "power" gifts: the gift of faith, the gifts of healing, and miraculous powers. Group Three is made up of the "speaking" or "inspiration" gifts: prophecy, different kinds of tongues, and the interpretation of tongues.

Each of these gifts involves a supernatural manifestation of the power of God. Everything God does is supernatural since that is his nature, but here we are looking at actual demonstrations of his presence and power. Let's consider each of them.

Group One: The "Knowing" or "Revelation" Gifts

1. The Message of Wisdom

The message of wisdom is a revelation given by the Holy Spirit of something known only to God. It will often point to the future, to something in the purpose or plan of God, and will address the needs of a person or situation. It may come to us through a vision, a dream, an inner conviction, or perhaps through prophecy or a message in tongues with an interpretation. A message of wisdom has nothing to do with our intellectual capacity, nor is it linked to the sort of worldly wisdom that enables us to deal with the affairs of life or to give wise counsel. It applies God's wisdom to a particular situation in a way that is beyond our natural ability.

An example from the Book of Acts is Peter's vision of the unclean food he was instructed to eat and his subsequent journey to the house of the Gentile, Cornelius (Acts 10:9-48). God gives Peter a vision that reveals something totally contrary to the way Peter understands the law: first, eating food that is ritually unclean; then, giving hospitality to Gentiles and entering the house of a Gentile; and finally, preaching the gospel to the Gentiles—none of which would be accepted by a good Jew. So God prepares him in a vision for what is going to happen, knowing it is completely outside of Peter's way of thinking. Through this miraculous revelation of his will and his plan, God prepares Peter for what he will be facing shortly.

2. *The Message of Knowledge*

This is very similar to the message of wisdom in that it, too, is a supernatural revelation given by the Holy Spirit of something in the mind of God. It usually relates to the present or the past rather than to the future.

God has all knowledge; he is omniscient, but he does not reveal everything to us. Sometimes he just reveals a simple fact or perhaps just a word, because this is enough to uncover the truth, to open a door, or to point to a solution. Again, it is not something we have learned intellectually or as the result of special study but something God reveals to us at a particular moment. It is neither a human ability nor a psychic experience.

An example in the New Testament is the meeting of Jesus and the Samaritan woman at the well of Sychar in chapter 4 of the Gospel of John. In verse 18, Jesus tells the woman she has had five husbands—knowledge given to him by the Holy Spirit. As a result, she sees Jesus as a prophet and listens even more intently to what he has to say. Similarly, in Acts, Peter knows by the Holy Spirit that Ananias and Sapphira have lied and kept back some of their money instead of giving all of it to the apostles for distribution to those in need. This message of knowledge has a very dramatic effect when he announces it (5:3-5)!

The message of knowledge, the message of wisdom, and prophetic insights often operate together. While they are distinct gifts, we must avoid worrying about exactly which gift is being given and just follow the prompting of the Spirit. All three of them convey to us, through the power of the Holy Spirit, something God wants us to know for the benefit of one person, of a group, or sometimes of many people—even a whole community.

3. The Distinguishing between Spirits

This is a gift involving supernatural insight into the world of all spirits—the Holy Spirit, demons, satanic spirits, and the human spirit. It is the supernatural ability to distinguish the good or evil tendencies in a spirit, or the good or evil power behind a spiritual manifestation. It is not thought reading, psychological insight, or any kind of mind game, and it is limited to a single group of beings—spirits. Even without the gift of distinguishing between spirits, we may often have an inner sense that something is not of God, particularly if we know his word and are walking closely with him. But this supernatural gift enables us to recognize with certainty when a spirit is at work and to react to the situation as the Holy Spirit directs us.

St. Paul reminds us that "our struggle is not against flesh and blood, but against the rulers, against the authorities, against the powers of this dark world and against the spiritual forces of evil in the heavenly realms" (Ephesians 6:12). It is in this struggle that the spiritual gift of distinguishing or discerning of spirits is of such importance. In his first letter, John reminds us, "Do not believe every spirit, but test the spirits to see whether they are from God" (1 John 4:1). And at a General Audience in Rome on November 15, 1972, Blessed Pope Paul VI said,

> Evil is not merely a lack of something, but an effective agent,
> a living spiritual being, perverted and perverting, a terrible

reality. It is contrary to the teaching of the Bible and the Church to refuse to recognize the existence of such a reality or to explain it as a pseudo-reality, a conceptual and fanciful personification of the unknown causes of our misfortunes. . . .

That it is not a question of one devil, but of many, as indicated by various passages in the Gospel (Luke 11:21; Mark 5:9). But the principal one is Satan, which means the adversary, the enemy; and with him many, all creatures of God, but fallen because of their rebellion and damnation. . . .

The question of the devil and the influence he can exert on individual persons, as well as on communities, whole societies, or events, is a very important chapter of Catholic doctrine that is given little attention today, though it should be studied again.[22]

In Acts 16, we find a slave girl who was possessed by an evil spirit and who told fortunes. She follows Paul, Luke, and Silas, shouting, "These men are servants of the Most High God, who are telling you the way to be saved!" (16:17). In the light of Paul's teaching in Ephesians 6, we can see how important it is to be protected against the deceptions of evil spirits by the gift of distinguishing between spirits. This is especially the case because evil spirits sometimes masquerade as angels of light—as in this example from Acts, when the spirit in the girl actually speaks the truth. Paul and his companions are servants of the Most High God, and they are telling people about salvation in Jesus. But Paul recognizes the presence of a false spirit and acts accordingly, saying to the spirit: "'In the name of Jesus Christ I command you to come out of her!' At that moment the spirit left her"(16:18).

This gift of discernment is the supernatural ability to know what is motivating a person to say or do something. There are three likely sources of this motivation: God the Holy Spirit, a demonic spirit, or the human spirit. We receive a really strong conviction that God is at work when something is said or done, or that it is not God at all but rather another spirit of some kind. Often it is just human thinking being expressed, which may be right or wrong, but sometimes there is clearly an evil spirit at work in a person, and that person needs to be set free from it. This will happen through a prayer of deliverance or, in extreme cases of possession, through a formal exorcism.

Group Two: The "Doing" or "Power" Gifts

4. The Gift of Faith

This gift of faith is given so that we can receive miracles. It is a total conviction that God is going to act in a supernatural way in a particular situation and that we need to speak or act in order to release his power. We have complete faith that what we are saying or doing is God's will and that he will honor our word or action and make it happen. So it is quite different from the faith that brings us into a relationship with God—believing in him and his plan of salvation. Neither is it the simple faith we exercise when we ask God to answer our prayers, and it has nothing to do with faithfulness, which grows in us as a fruit of the presence of the Holy Spirit. Hebrews 11:1 reminds us, "Now faith is confidence in what we hope for and assurance about what we do not see." This gift makes us certain about something we cannot yet see.

Elijah's challenge to the prophets of Baal on Mount Carmel is an amazing example of this gift of faith in action. God gave Elijah the absolute certainty that he would work a remarkable miracle, but first Elijah had to act (1 Kings 18). So with complete faith in God, he sets the scene, issues the challenge, and then plays his part in the total destruction of God's enemies. The key point is that Elijah had to step out in faith and issue the challenge in order that God might be vindicated.

5. Gifts of Healing

What we are dealing with here is the supernatural curing of physical, psychological, and emotional diseases—God intervening and bringing healing to a sick person. The healings come from God who works through a person who prays or asks for the healing. Healing prayer is an important part of Catholic tradition; answers to prayers for healing have occurred throughout the history of the Church. These gifts of healings are not medical treatments of any sort but direct interventions by the Holy Spirit. In the Letter of James, we read, "Is anyone among you sick? Let them call the elders of the church to pray over them and anoint them with oil in the name of the Lord. And the prayer offered in faith will make the sick person well; the Lord will raise them up" (5:14-15).

This is what we are all called to do, and while we may not understand why the Lord heals some people and not others, we do know that sometimes through prayer or a word of command, a person is amazingly healed, and we describe this as a gift of healing. Since healing can be controversial, I will deal with this gift in more detail.

Paul never describes people as "healers" because no one possesses a habitual gift of healing, but there are people who receive a special charism for healing. This doesn't mean they possess the ability to heal whenever they want to but that God often uses them as instruments for his healing power. Every single healing is a gift from God, as each one is an individual encounter with the Lord of love and power.

In the four Gospels, there are 41 specific instances of healings, while 727 verses (about a fifth of the Gospels) are devoted to the subject of healings. Why did Jesus give so much emphasis to healing? When Jesus heals, it's a sign that the kingdom of God is present. His purpose was not only to restore a person to health and wholeness but to bring about the kingdom where God reigns. Healings reinforced his message of salvation and forgiveness, and he passed this ministry on to his followers, giving his disciples authority to heal in his name: "Jesus called his twelve disciples to him and gave them authority to drive out impure spirits and to heal every disease and sickness" (Matthew 10:1). His final act before his ascension was to send his disciples out into the whole world to preach the good news, which was to be accompanied by signs, including healings: "They will place their hands on sick people, and they will get well" (Mark 16:18).

An example of this gift is found in Acts, when Peter heals the crippled beggar at the Beautiful Gate of the Temple (3:1-10). Later in Acts, Luke writes, "Crowds gathered also from the towns around Jerusalem, bringing their sick and those tormented by impure spirits, and all of them were healed" (5:16). The disciples were exercising the gifts of healing they had been given.

In 2000, the Church's Congregation for the Doctrine of the Faith published a short document, *Instruction on Prayers for Healing,* which presents a very positive view of the gifts of healing and the healing ministry, together with some guidelines on liturgical services of healing. It encourages all of us to pray for healings and reminds us that "not only is it praiseworthy for individual members of the faithful to ask for healing for themselves and for others, but the Church herself asks the Lord for the health of the sick in her liturgy."[23]

Everywhere people are looking for healing and wholeness, not just physical, spiritual, and emotional healing, but healing in our society and between nations and races. The following words from Anglican Bishop Morris Maddocks remind us that healing is all about Jesus. With the proliferation of New Age practices and other spiritualities, his advice is timely:

Christian healing is, first and foremost, about Christ. It follows the pattern he set in his own ministry and the commission he gave to his own disciples. The fact that it happens at all is the fruit of his work, both in the creation and salvation of mankind. In both these mighty works, humankind has been created and re-created in the image of God—has been made whole. It is the whole work of Christ in a person's body, mind, and spirit designed to bring that person to that wholeness which is God's will for us.[24]

We should all pray for the healing of sick people, and sometimes we will receive a supernatural gift of healing, meaning that the Lord will use us as his instruments to bring healing to a person. Some people will be used regularly in this way, and it will be said that they exercise "a ministry of healing," but still, healing will only happen when God releases the gift.

6. Miraculous Powers

A miracle is a supernatural intervention in the ordinary course of nature: a temporary suspension or alteration of the natural order, brought about by the power of the Holy Spirit. In one sense, all God's workings are miraculous, but what we are dealing with here is a specific supernatural act on the natural plane. Miraculous powers are a wonderful gift glorifying God, stimulating faith, and astonishing an unbelieving world.

The Scriptures are full of examples: the miracles performed by Moses in front of Pharaoh (Exodus 7–11), the parting of the Red Sea (Exodus 14), Jesus turning water into wine (John 2:1-11), the feeding of the five thousand (6:5-15), and many more. In all these examples, the natural order was temporarily suspended and the miraculous power of God took over, with amazing results.

Group Three: The "Speaking" or "Inspiration" Gifts

7. Prophecy

Sometimes God speaks to us very directly. He chooses certain people and uses them as his mouthpieces. They speak words directly to individuals, to communities, even to nations. The gift of prophecy is speaking a message from God inspired by the Holy Spirit. It does not add to the deposit of faith but shows that God is present and speaking to us. Every Christian shares in the prophetic office of Christ and is called to be a witness to the gospel message in word and deed, but what we are addressing here is different: it's a special grace given for a particular time and place.

In the simple gift of prophecy, there is no revelation—just words of encouragement, edification, or comfort. As St. Paul explains, "The one who prophesies speaks to people for their strengthening, encouraging and comfort" (1 Corinthians 14:3). This simple gift is available to everyone, which is why Paul writes, "Eagerly desire gifts of the Spirit, especially the gift of prophecy" (14:1). We should always be prepared for God to use us in this way.

But there is more to prophecy than just the simple gift of encouragement. The Old Testament prophets and John the Baptist, often described as the last of the Old Testament prophets, were specially chosen by God and given a ministry of bringing his word to the people, often foretelling future events and warning of what was to come. There are several Old Testament accounts of the calling of prophets (Isaiah 6; Jeremiah 1; Ezekiel 2–3). Here we find men who were specifically called by God and then sent to speak his word to the people. After John the Baptist, "a man sent from God" (John 1:6), we still find men and women with a prophetic ministry who foretell future events. This ministry of the prophet is listed in Romans 12:6 and in Ephesians 4:11, along with apostles, leaders, teachers, pastors, and evangelists.

It is clear that these are all special callings that become a major part of a person's life, and so they are not the same as a simple gift. When Jesus himself is rejected in Nazareth, he remarks, "No prophet is accepted in his hometown" (Luke

4:24). He also teaches us that "whoever welcomes a prophet as a prophet will receive a prophet's reward" (Matthew 10:41). Perhaps we are surprised that "God has placed in the Church first of all apostles, second prophets" (1 Corinthians 12:28). The ministry of a prophet is obviously seen by God as being very important.

In Acts we have the example of a man named Agabus giving Paul an acted-out prophecy:

> A prophet named Agabus came down from Judea. Coming over to us, he took Paul's belt, tied his own hands and feet with it and said, "The Holy Spirit says, 'In this way the Jewish leaders in Jerusalem will bind the owner of this belt and will hand him over to the Gentiles.'" (Acts 21:10-11)

Agabus, inspired by the Spirit, came a long way to deliver this graphic prophetic word to prepare Paul for what would happen to him in Jerusalem. He also prophesied that a severe famine was coming, and in response, the church in Antioch sent relief to the brethren in Judea (Acts 11:27-30). Others with this special ministry are Judas, called Barsabbas, and Silas (15:32). In Luke, the eighty-four-year-old widow, Anna, is described as "a prophet" (2:36). The ministry of a prophet was clearly greatly valued in the early church.

But there are many others who give prophetic words without being recognized as having specific callings to be prophets to the people, and there is evidence in the New Testament that this simpler gift was common in the early Christian communities. In fact, Paul's reason for writing about the spiritual gifts in his first letter to the Corinthians was to correct some abuses that had crept into the church, with too many people prophetically giving public words of encouragement and speaking out in tongues.

One example of a number of people prophesying is found in Acts, when Paul baptizes twelve men into the name of the Lord Jesus. As he lays his hands on them, "The Holy Spirit came on them, and they spoke in tongues and prophesied" (Acts 19:6). There is no suggestion here that they are called to be prophets, so we may assume they are giving simple prophetic words for "strengthening, encouraging and comfort," as Paul describes it in 1 Corinthians 14:3. In his discussion of prophecy in this chapter, Paul encourages the Corinthian Christians to "eagerly desire gifts of the Spirit, especially prophecy" (14:1) and in verse 5 says, "I would like every one of you to speak in tongues, but I would rather have you prophesy." This is clearly not about everyone having the special calling to be a prophet but about bringing prophetic words of exhortation and encouragement to the assembled community.

So when it comes to prophecy, there is the simple gift and there is the special calling to a ministry; both are important, and we must take them seriously. Recognized prophets will also often exercise the more simple gift of exhortation, encouragement, and strengthening as shown in Acts, when "Judas and Silas, who themselves were prophets, said much to encourage and strengthen the brothers" (15:32).

But prophets will sometimes be wrong, so every prophetic word needs to be tested. This is primarily the responsibility of the leaders, with the help of other prophets: "Two or three prophets should speak, and the others should weigh carefully what is said" (1 Corinthians 14:29).

It is clear from Scripture that prophets come under the authority of the apostles. "In the church God has placed first of all apostles, second prophets, third teachers" (1 Corinthians 12:28). But it is also important to note that the Church is "built on the foundations of the apostles and prophets, with Christ Jesus himself as the chief cornerstone" (Ephesians 2:20). Prophets have a very important ministry in the Church.

Only in Matthew's Gospel do we find this specific and rather dramatic warning of Jesus against the false prophets who will infiltrate his followers: "Watch out for false prophets. They come to you in sheep's clothing, but inwardly they are ferocious wolves. By their fruit you will recognize them" (7:15-6).

I think we can safely say that he was thinking of those who would come with distorted versions of the gospel, false claims to be the true messiah, or with a desire to cause disunity and lead people astray. But it is a timely warning of the need for testing and discernment, and an important part of this "weighing" is the life and moral standing of the person who delivers the prophetic word—the prophet himself.

With this goes the orthodoxy of the word itself and what it says about Jesus. St. John reminds us, "This is how you can recognize the Spirit of God: Every spirit that acknowledges that Jesus Christ has come in the flesh is from God, but every spirit that does not acknowledge Jesus is not from God" (1 John 4:2-3). Paul echoes this point: "Therefore I want you to know that no one who is speaking by the Spirit of God says, 'Jesus be cursed,' and no one can say, 'Jesus is Lord,' except by the Holy Spirit" (1 Corinthians 12:3).

In conclusion, it is important to remind ourselves that the style in which the prophetic word is delivered should not be a primary element in discerning its authenticity. In Scripture we can find examples of strange words, dreams, pictures, visions, actions, and unusual physical demonstrations. Any prophecy should, however, always be in line with Scripture and Church teaching and be upbuilding even if it is challenging. A true word from God will always be life-giving. A question we might ask today is this one: "Are there prophets in our church congregations, and are they encouraged to speak out; or is this a gift we need to stir up again?"

8. Different Kinds of Tongues

Speaking in tongues is a supernatural utterance inspired by the Holy Spirit in words the speaker has never learned and does not understand. It is a simple and basic gift but the one people often find the most difficult to accept. It is probably the strangest of the spiritual gifts.

Its primary use is in our private prayer life so that we can praise and worship God freely without the limitation of using words we understand and may feel are inadequate. In this usage, it is the only spiritual gift not given for the benefit of others, although in a certain way, the fact that my personal relationship with God is strengthened will be a benefit to the wider community. God gives us this gift so that we can speak to him from our hearts in total freedom.

The mind can act as a dam when the "rivers of living water" pour out from our hearts (John 7:38), so when we need to overflow with praise, God provides a temporary bypass through the gift of speaking in tongues. Paul tells us, "For anyone who speaks in a tongue does not speak to people but to God" (1 Corinthians 14:2). I have personally found the gift of tongues to be the one thing that has been the greatest benefit in my own daily private prayer.

Like every gift from God, speaking in tongues should be desired and actively sought, but like the other gifts, not everyone receives it. "Do all speak in tongues?" (1 Corinthians 12:30) implies that not everyone will speak in tongues, and this is consistent with our understanding of how gifts are given: to one this gift, to another that gift. Some classical Pentecostals regard speaking in tongues as the only acceptable evidence that someone has been baptized in the Holy Spirit, but this is not the view held by Catholics and most Protestants.

In 1 Corinthians 14, Paul seems to give almost contradictory teaching on this gift. In verse 5 he says, "I would like every one of you to speak in tongues, but I would rather have you prophesy," and then in verse 18 he writes, "I thank God that I speak in tongues more than all of you." It becomes clear, if we read 1 Corinthians 14:1-25, that Paul is mainly dealing with speaking in tongues in public services, and is making the point that public messages in tongues do not edify others because, unless they are interpreted, they are unintelligible. Prophetic words, however, bring encouragement that edifies the congregation. This is why I explained that speaking in tongues is primarily for our private prayer times, as this is quite clearly the view of Paul. It seems there was disorder and confusion in the public meetings of the church at Corinth, with many people speaking out in tongues at the same time, and Paul was laying down some basic rules for good order.

Since the gift of speaking in tongues is primarily for our private prayer, it will have a limited expression in public gatherings of the community. So public utterances in tongues should be few and should always be interpreted so that everyone will understand the message. There is one exception or variation to this: singing in tongues.

Today we often experience singing in tongues, when people in a public gathering or service spontaneously begin to use the gift of tongues in song in a most beautiful melody and harmony given by the Holy Spirit. It can only be described as inspired praise and worship of God. Because it is addressed to God, no interpretation is to be expected. It is spontaneous and harmonious, and it fades away as suddenly as it has begun. Pope Francis is clearly personally familiar with this aspect of the gift of tongues. Addressing fifty thousand charismatic Catholics in Rome's Olympic Stadium in June 2014, he noted, "When I celebrated Mass in the cathedral in Buenos Aires with the charismatic renewal, after the consecration and after a few seconds of adoration in tongues, we would sing this hymn with great joy and fervor, as you have today."[25]

Paul assumes that anyone can control the use of their gift of speaking in tongues. It is not an ecstatic utterance that overtakes us, causing us to lose rational control of our actions. When the gift of speaking in tongues is used, it is never out of our control—we can stop speaking whenever we wish. As one pastor explained it, "The idea that a speaker in tongues goes off into a kind of religious ecstasy, where he loses both emotional and personal control, is contrary both to Scripture and actual experience. The person who exercises this gift is perfectly able to remain in full control of himself and his emotions."

In addition to chapters 12 and 14 of Paul's first letter to the Corinthians, the gift of tongues is mentioned in Acts.

When the Holy Spirit came upon the household of Cornelius, "they heard them speaking in tongues and praising God" (Acts 10:46), and in Ephesus, "when Paul placed his hands on them, the Holy Spirit came on them, and they spoke in tongues and prophesied" (19:6). The gift of tongues is certainly a sign of the presence of the Holy Spirit, and this is one reason Paul encourages us to seek it.

But our understanding of the normal use of the gift of tongues should be based on the practical teaching of Paul in 1 Corinthians 12–14, as we know that Paul spoke in tongues himself and had firsthand experience of the value and use of the gift. It is also clear from St. Paul's teaching that in its normal usage, the gift of tongues is unintelligible both to the speaker and to the hearers, which forms the basis for his clear assertion that when used publicly, it is inferior to the gift of prophecy, which everyone can understand. He explains his thinking: "Since you are eager for the gifts of the Spirit, try to excel in those that build up the church. For this reason the one who speaks in a tongue should pray that they may interpret what they say" (14:12-13). This also strengthens his view that tongues are primarily a gift for private prayer: "For anyone who speaks in a tongue does not speak to people but to God. Indeed, no one understands them; they utter mysteries by the Spirit" (14:2).

People are sometimes confused about the gift of tongues when they read how it was given to the disciples in a particular way at Pentecost: "When they heard this sound, a crowd came together in bewilderment, because each one heard their own language being spoken" (Acts 2:6). Experience shows that a tongue in the language of a listener is quite rare today, although this was clearly the experience of the crowds on Pentecost Day. But in 1 Corinthians 12–14, we have Paul's reliable teaching on the ways the gift of tongues is normally used: in our private prayer, and occasionally in a public meeting with an interpretation. The Pentecost Day experience of the gift clearly demonstrated the presence of the Holy Spirit and caught the crowd's attention, as many languages not known to the disciples were spoken. Our experience today is that just occasionally, a public message given in tongues may be in a language that someone present knows, but usually such a message will require interpretation.

In concluding the section on this unusual gift, I offer St. Teresa of Avila's experience, as described in her book *The Interior Castle*:

Our Lord sometimes gives the soul feelings of jubilation and a strange prayer it doesn't understand. I am writing about this favor here so that if He grants it to you, you may give Him much praise and know what is taking place. It is, in my opinion, a deep union of the faculties; but our Lord nonetheless leaves them free that they might enjoy this joy—and the same goes for the senses—without understanding what it is they are enjoying or how they are enjoying. What I'm saying seems like gibberish, but certainly the experience takes place in this way, for the joy is so excessive the soul wouldn't want to enjoy it alone but wants to tell everyone about it so that they might help this soul praise our Lord. All its activity is directed to this praise. [26]

Similarly, St. Augustine describes it like this:

One who jubilates does not utter words but a certain sound of joy without words; for it is the voice of the soul poured forth in joy, expressing as far as possible what it feels without reflecting on the meaning. . . . If you cannot express your joy, jubilate; jubilation expresses your joy if you cannot speak. Let not your joy be silent. [27]

St. Gregory the Great puts it this way:

We call it *jubilus* when we conceive such joy in the heart as we cannot give vent to by the force of words, and yet the triumph of the heart vents with the voice what it cannot give forth by speech. Now the mouth is rightly said to be filled with laughter, the lips with jubilation, since in that eternal land when the mind of the righteous is borne away in transport, the tongue is lifted up in the song of praise.[28]

This sounds very much like what Paul writes about in Ephesians 5:19-20: "[Speak] to one another with psalms, hymns, and songs from the Spirit. Sing and make music from your heart to the Lord, always giving thanks to God the Father for everything."

9. *The Interpretation of Tongues*

This is the supernatural interpretation, into a language known to the hearers, of the meaning of a message delivered in tongues. It is an interpretation, not a direct translation. The purpose is clearly to render the gift of tongues intelligible so that the hearers may all be edified. Interpretation is important when the message is given in tongues at a public meeting; it is not required for our private prayer in tongues. When someone begins to speak publicly in tongues, another person will be given the gift of interpretation and will immediately be open to the guidance of the Holy Spirit so that they are available to bring the interpretation when inspired to do so. The interpretation is sometimes given by the same person who spoke out in tongues, something referred to by St. Paul: "The one who speaks in a tongue should pray that they may interpret what they say" (1 Corinthians 14:13).

As we have already seen, the New Testament teaching on the interpretation of tongues is to be found in 1 Corinthians 14, where Paul gives examples of good and bad practices. When a message in tongues is given in a public meeting or service and then is interpreted by someone in the congregation, the effect is to powerfully focus the attention of all who are present on what God is saying.

Stirrings of the Holy Spirit

We have looked at the charisms listed in 1 Corinthians 12, which are also known as special spiritual graces. One thing we need to remember is that in this context, our use of the word "spiritual" has a particular meaning that relates it directly to the Holy Spirit. We do not just mean supernatural because, as we know from Ephesians 6, there are many other supernatural powers and spirits in the heavenly realms.

A message of knowledge or wisdom, a prophetic word, a gift of faith or healing—these can change a person's life in a moment, in a way that years of therapy or treatment may never achieve. When someone is instantly healed of an obvious sickness, when the blind see or the lame walk, we are immediately aware that God is at work among us. We need God's help to challenge the things that are wrong in our society and to bring wholeness and freedom to people who are suffering. This is why we must always be open to the work of the Spirit and be willing to be used as channels for his gifts.

Perhaps St. Hilary of Poitiers can have the last word:

> We who have been reborn through the Sacrament of Baptism experience intense joy when we feel within us the first stirrings of the Holy Spirit. We begin to have insight into the mysteries of faith; we are able to prophesy and speak with wisdom. We become steadfast in hope and receive abundant gifts of healing. Demons are made subject to our authority. These gifts enter us like a gentle rain, and . . . little by little, they bear abundant fruit.[29]

None of these gifts are delegated to us by higher Church authorities. We receive them because we are baptized and open to the Holy Spirit. Entry into the spiritual gifts comes when we are willing to let the Holy Spirit use us. It's as simple as that—we just need the courage to pray, *"Come, Holy Spirit!"*

Questions for Reflection and Discussion

1. Charisms or special gifts are supernatural, given or inspired by the Holy Spirit as he chooses, and may be given to anyone who has received the Holy Spirit and is open to the charisms. Are you familiar with them? If not, why do you think this is? What needs to happen to make the charisms better understood and more widely used?

2. Explain and discuss the purpose of each of the nine gifts listed. Which one do you most desire?

3. What does the Church say and teach today about these supernatural gifts of the Holy Spirit? Is this teaching generally known and understood in your parish?

4. Pope St. John Paul II encouraged us to seek these special gifts or charisms. Why do you think he wanted them for us?

Helpful Scripture passages to pray:
   1 Corinthians 12:7-10
   Romans 12:6-8
   Ephesians 4:11-12
   1 Peter 4:10

CHAPTER FIVE

The Gifts of the Holy Spirit in Practice

1. Why do we need the spiritual gifts?
2. What do we mean by "spiritual"?
3. How are we to use these gifts of the Spirit?

1. Why do we need the spiritual gifts?

We need the gifts of the Holy Spirit just as much today as in the early church, but sadly, few people even know they are available. All these gifts and ministries of the Holy Spirit, as well as others we have not considered, contribute to the basic mission to love, care, share, and serve, to which every Christian is called. Today we may be much more sophisticated than the early Christians and know more about many things, but there are still physical, mental, and emotional needs that can only be met in the power of the Spirit.

What is needed is the realization that all the spiritual gifts are still available today to those who open their lives to the presence and power of the Holy Spirit. The spiritual gifts we have been considering are given to build up our faith, to bring wholeness to different areas of our lives, to show that we are a community dependent on one another, and to bring glory to God through the extension of his kingdom. We need to

116

understand the gifts and recognize their importance, praying that the Holy Spirit will pour them out among us.

2. What do we mean by "spiritual"?

By "spiritual" we mean

- of the Holy Spirit;
- in the Holy Spirit;
- formed by the Holy Spirit;
- by the power of the Holy Spirit;
- with the character of the Holy Spirit;
- showing the fruit of the Holy Spirit.

We are studying gifts that come to us from God to help us build up the Christian community, meet individual needs, and become more effective witnesses to the message of the gospel and the person of Jesus Christ.

St. Paul reminds us, "There are different kinds of gifts, but the same Spirit distributes them. There are different kinds of service, but the same Lord. There are different kinds of working, but in all of them and in everyone it is the same God at work" (1 Corinthians 12:4-6). Later in that chapter, he adds, "Just as a body, though one, has many parts, but all its many parts form one body, so it is with Christ" and "Even so the body is not made up of one part but of many" (verses 12, 14). Finally, he writes, "Now you are the body of Christ, and each one of you is a part of it" (verse 27).

These Scripture passages remind us that although we are all different, we are in this together. We need each other;

we are interdependent. So my gift is for you and your gift is for me. We may pray for specific gifts for ourselves, but we need to accept that the very nature of any gift is that it is not earned or merited but is freely given as the Giver decides, not as the recipient demands. Above all, it is the Giver we seek, not just his gifts.

It is wonderful to receive these amazing gifts and to be used by God to bring his wholeness to others, but we must use them only as he requires and always under the guidance of the Holy Spirit. We do not possess them; they are his, and we are merely the instruments he chooses to bring his life-changing power to others. The answer to our next question will help us see how this works when it comes to exercising the gifts of the Holy Spirit.

3. So how are we to use these gifts of the Holy Spirit?

We have seen that the gifts of the Holy Spirit are not given to us for our private benefit but for the good of all of us. They are available to anyone who has decided to give the Spirit freedom to work in and through them. Paul emphasizes that these special gifts are given to build up the faith and spiritual power of the church community so that others will be drawn to share in the joy and abundant life they see before them. They are, therefore, tools to build up the body rather than an end to be sought in and of themselves.

We have considered the list of individual gifts given by Paul in 1 Corinthians 12, and we have briefly looked at some of his instructions on how they are to be used, which we find in chapter 14. It is hardly a coincidence that between these two chapters, we find in chapter 13 Paul's great teaching on love.

Taken in its context, 1 Corinthians 13 is really about gifts plus love, an illustration rather than an exhortation. The exhortation follows in the first sentence of chapter 14: "Follow the way of love and eagerly desire gifts of the Spirit." In chapter 13, Paul is telling us to be practical about love—it's not just some vague feeling or emotional response; it's about how we behave at home, at work, in the grocery store, in our places of leisure, in our church. The good way is to know all about the gifts God wants us to have—the excellent way is to use those gifts in an atmosphere of love: "I will show you the most excellent way" (12:31).

"God is love" (1 John 4:8, 16), and the gifts of the Spirit come from God. In themselves they are good gifts from a loving God, but the manifestation of them will reveal the love or lack of love in a church, group, or community. Today we may think we have love, but often that's not really true. We meet each other on a rather superficial and polite level, and it's easy to maintain a good relationship at arm's length. But let us get close, involved, and mixed up in each other's day-to-day lives, and we'll soon discover how strong our love really is. As Jesus reminds us, "By this everyone will know that you are my disciples, if you love one another" (John 13:35), and the author of Hebrews exhorts us to "keep on loving one other" (13:1).

Exercising any charism is an act of love.
In 1 Corinthians 13, Paul tells us that

- love is patient;
- love bears all things;
- love always believes the best;
- love endures;
- love keeps on loving;
- love holds on even when I let people down again and again;
- love always hopes for the best.

So how do we stand up to the test of this love that is so essential, the heart of the message of Christianity, a reflection of the very nature of God? It's not just a matter of how we feel—it involves our will. It's an *agape* love that deliberately chooses its object and continues to love through thick and thin. It will dominate not just our emotions and intellect but also our will. Christianity is the only religion that says, "God is love" (1 John 4:8, 16), and when you and I love, we become more like God. The gifts of the Holy Spirit are given to us by a loving God and are to be used in a climate of love. Just as a human body needs lubricating fluid to help it function, so the Church, the body of Christ, needs love to make it function properly.

Our claims to be full of the Holy Spirit are meaningless if our attitudes and behavior do not show love. It's the first fruit that grows in us, demonstrating that the Holy Spirit is present and at work. Gifts and ministries are dangerous and ineffective without love. What do I mean by this?

Building up the body

The gifts of the Spirit are given to build up the body of Christ, and this includes our local church. When Paul wrote his first letter to the Corinthians, he was sending a pastoral letter to a local church with instructions on how to do things properly. Now, we all know what it means to be part of a local church: the joys and sorrows, the encouragements and frustrations, the cliques and factions, the progressives and the conservatives, the passionate and the lukewarm, the friendly and the aloof—all presided over by the priest or pastor who is trying to listen to the Lord, preach his word, celebrate the sacraments, give some direction, and keep everything going.

In this complex mix, we should find the gifts of the Holy Spirit being used. The fact that this may not normally be our experience simply means that we are not living in the fullness of what God intends for us, and we may not have the right priorities. When there is genuine love, when relationships are good, and when a parish is moving forward, the gifts will be given and received with thanksgiving and will bear fruit. Where there is little love and no real vision, we will find jealousy, disagreement, and division—soil in which the fruit cannot grow and in which we are not likely to find the gifts of the Holy Spirit being freely used.

This is why St. Paul teaches us that love is so important in using the gifts.

- Love is harmony, not division.
- Love is humility, not arrogance.
- Love builds; it does not destroy.
- Love is sensitive, not overbearing.

- Love means being willing to restrict my liberty for the sake of another.

The gifts of the Spirit will test our love for one another. When I know that you love me, I will accept almost anything from you, and so the Lord can use you to minister to me. If I'm not sure that you love me, I will be hesitant about receiving anything from you.

God often gives spiritual gifts to young, immature Christians; he knows they'll usually have the courage to step out in faith and use the gifts. But this may provoke jealousy in more mature Christians, who may wonder, "Why has God given her that gift when I've been faithful for all these years and she's only been here for five minutes?" We need to remember that the gifts speak about the Giver and the beneficiary, not about the instrument, and they are given to build up the church community. The exercise of the gifts of the Spirit does not depend on a person being mature, holy, or even in a state of grace. But if the gifts are to be fully effective, they must always be used in love. So the most important part of the answer to our question "How are we to use these gifts of the Holy Spirit?" is to use them in love.

And in good order

Paul then goes on to tell us that these must also be used in an orderly way: "When you come together, each of you has a hymn, or a word of instruction, a revelation, a tongue or an interpretation. Everything must be done so that the church may be built up" (1 Corinthians 14:26). In the early church, it seems that people came together bursting to give. They were so stirred up by the Holy Spirit that they needed rules to maintain order and stop the meeting from getting out of control—hardly our problem today!

Paul is teaching the Corinthians in chapter 14 that there must always be

- sensitivity to those around us;
- sensitivity to the glory of God;
- a limiting of the gifts at times to maintain good order;
- testing of the gifts by others;
- respect for authority and Church structure;
- cooperation with the Holy Spirit;
- cooperation within the body;
- submission to the lordship of Jesus;
- submission to the authority of Scripture;
- submission to the teaching authority of the Church.

As St. Paul reminds us, "God is not a God of disorder but of peace" (1 Corinthians 14:33) and "Everything should be done in a fitting and orderly way" (14:40). This means that I must restrain my gift if it cannot be made edifying to the church assembly, and I must restrain my participation according to biblical teaching on the functions and relationships between members of the Church. I must only use my gift in accordance with the teaching of Scripture and under the authority of the local leadership. It is one thing to receive an inspiration from the Holy Spirit. It is quite another thing to know when and how to use it. This is something the Lord will teach us, often through our leaders and mentors. To use the spiritual gifts properly and effectively, we need faith, love, time, and good order.

Tools for a job

God wants us to have the gifts of his Holy Spirit, so we must desire them and ask for them. He will not force them upon us, but without them we are impoverished and much more limited in our ability to meet the needs of those around us. The gifts are not going to come because we sit around and lament their absence. We need to teach about them and encourage people to ask for them in expectant faith. When God uses us as instruments to help others, our faith increases, we become more committed, and as a result, God can use us to even greater effect.

The gifts of the Holy Spirit are not some exotic, superspiritual novelties; they are for here and now, where we live and act—where we laugh, cry, love, work, and suffer. The gifts are tools for a job, and the job is to produce better fruit. We don't need a spade at the top of a tree—we need it down at the bottom in the mud. Gifts are not a sign of spiritual maturity, but fruit is, and we will move on to look at the fruit in the next chapter.

It is my hope that this chapter has provided a better understanding of the spiritual gifts—that we'll have realized why we need them and how we are to use them. Perhaps some of the ignorance to which Paul referred will have been dispelled. But the question is still there—do we want these gifts? If so, are we prepared to ask the Holy Spirit for them? And then, are we prepared to step out in faith and use them as he stirs them up within us, knowing that not everyone will agree with what we're doing? It takes courage to stand up for what we believe when we know we'll be challenged. If we're willing to step outside our comfort zones and follow God in faith, we will be tested. Every time we're prepared to stand for something or try something new, there will always be someone to tell us we're wrong. We need the courage of our convictions.

In the early church, the Pentecost experience of the presence and power of the Holy Spirit was very much alive, and candidates for baptism expected to receive charismatic gifts. This is clearly expressed by St. Cyril of Jerusalem: "My final words, beloved ones, in this instruction are words of exhortation, urging all of you to prepare your souls for the reception of the heavenly charisms."[30]

In May 1998, at a meeting of the ecclesial movements and new communities, Pope St. John Paul II exhorted us, "Open yourselves docilely to the gifts of the Spirit! Accept gratefully and obediently the charisms that the Spirit never ceases to bestow on us!"[31]

If we take the risk, ask for the gifts of the Holy Spirit, and then use them as the Spirit directs us, we'll reach heights we thought were beyond us. We'll see God at work, changing people's lives by his love and power and building up his Church.

Come, Holy Spirit!

Questions for Reflection and Discussion

1. Charisms are given to enrich the lives of all of us, to build up the Church, and to enable us to evangelize more effectively. How do they work in practice? Can we use one of these supernatural gifts whenever we choose to?

2. Have you personally received any of these gifts of the Holy Spirit? Have you exercised any of them, and if so, with what results?

3. How do the charisms help us evangelize?

4. How are we to use the gifts of the Holy Spirit in our groups or parishes?

Helpful Scripture passages to pray:
    1 Corinthians 12:4-6
    1 Corinthians 13–14
    John 13:35

CHAPTER SIX

The Fruit of the Holy Spirit

1. What is the fruit of the Holy Spirit?
2. The fruit of the Spirit is the nature of Jesus becoming more and more visible in our lives. What does this mean?
3. How is the fruit produced in our lives?
4. Why are we expected to bear fruit?

When we think of fruit, what comes to mind is something that appeals to our senses. We may see images of plants, bushes, and trees, all bearing different kinds, colors, shapes, and textures of fruit. We'll all have our favorites; fruit is something that is attractive and delicious. We don't make fruit in a factory—it grows, and good fruit is a clear sign of a good, healthy bush or tree.

1. What is the fruit of the Holy Spirit?

In Galatians, Paul describes the fruit of the Spirit in these words: "But the fruit of the Spirit is love, joy, peace, forbearance [patience], kindness, goodness, faithfulness, gentleness and self-control. Against such things there is no law" (5:22-23). To express it in a very simple way, the fruit listed are a display of the character of God himself, as revealed to us in the person of Jesus, his Son, during his time on earth. It's what should result from the new life of Christ, born in us at our baptism and present through the indwelling Holy Spirit.

When this kind of fruit is evident in our lives, it shows that through God's grace, the sanctifying power of the Holy Spirit is working in us—that we are good "trees" bearing ripe fruit. Jesus reminds us, "A good tree cannot bear bad fruit, and a bad tree cannot bear good fruit" (Matthew 7:18).

The fruit of the spirit are the good and attractive qualities that God produces in us, reflecting his goodness to us. They originate in his action within us that produces new life, creating a new relationship with him, with ourselves, and with our neighbor. Such a new relationship has no pretense or superficiality because it comes from something real: true love, joy, peace, patience, kindness, goodness, faithfulness, gentleness, and self-control. When these qualities can be seen, then clearly the Holy Spirit is at work and others will recognize the presence and power of God in us. "By their fruit you will recognize them," as Jesus tells us (Matthew 7:16).

The gifts of the Spirit and the fruit of the Spirit are quite distinct and different:

- the gifts of the Holy Spirit enable us to do what Jesus did while the fruit of the Spirit enables us to be like Jesus was;
- the gifts are many, while the fruit is one—the divine nature;
- the gifts are expressed corporately, while the fruit is shown individually.

Fruit is the clearest outward sign of the Holy Spirit's presence; the gifts are tools to help us produce fruit.

2. The fruit of the Spirit is the nature of Jesus becoming more evident in our lives. What exactly do we mean by this?

The list of the fruit of the Spirit consists of everything we would like to be: loving, joyful, peaceful, patient, kind, good, faithful, gentle, and self-controlled. I think it helps if we think of it as the nature of Jesus: one fruit with nine distinct flavors. If people see these qualities in us, they are seeing the character and personality of Jesus Christ. So let's take a brief look at each flavor:

Love comes first, because without it the other eight "flavors" would not exist. It's the new commandment of Jesus: "Love one another" (John 13:34). It is "the most excellent way" (1 Corinthians 12:31). It is entirely giving: "For God so loved the world that he gave his one and only Son" (John 3:16).

Joy is exciting and liberating. Knowing Christ fills us with "an inexpressible and glorious joy" (1 Peter 1:8) that others should see, "for the joy of the LORD is your strength" (cf. Nehemiah 8:10).

Peace is calmness, security, harmony, wholeness, completeness, assurance—God's supernatural rest in the midst of confusion and difficulties. While it is a flavor of the fruit of the Spirit (Galatians 5:22), it is also a gift from Christ: "Peace I leave with you; my peace I give you" (John 14:27).

Patience is self-restraint, tolerance, endurance, long-tempered-ness: "The LORD is gracious and compassionate, / slow to anger and rich in love" (Psalm 145:8). Our patience is based on the indisputable fact that God is at work in our lives.

Kindness is compassion, sympathy, mellowness, a quality that comes from the heart. "Be kind and compassionate to one another" (Ephesians 4:32).

Goodness is unstinted generosity, a way to express love in action. It means being generous with our time and posses-sions. God is good and so are his actions: "You are good, and what you do is good" (Psalm 119:68). In the same way, our goodness should be seen in our actions.

Faithfulness is complete trust, unquestioning belief, reliabil-ity, confidence; it's what the Christian life is all about. God has shown himself to be faithful and to keep his promises, so we know we can put our faith in him. God is looking for faithfulness, not necessarily success as we would see it. "Well done, good and faithful servant! You have been faithful with a few things; I will put you in charge of many things" (Mat-thew 25:21).

Gentleness is humility, lack of pride, meekness, not being resentful. Jesus explains it like this: "Take my yoke upon you and learn from me, for I am gentle and humble in heart, and you will find rest for your souls" (Matthew 11:29). Or as St Paul puts it, "If someone is caught in a sin, you who live by the Spirit should restore that person gently" (Galatians 6:1).

Self-control is the last in the list. It is self-restraint, moderation, temperance; it binds together all the other "flavors" of the fruit of the Spirit and shows that God is at work in our lives. In today's world, where consumerism and individualism are so prevalent, self-control is difficult and often less valued. But Paul tells us, "The grace of God . . . teaches us to say 'No' to ungodliness and worldly passions, and to live self-controlled, upright and godly lives in this present age" (Titus 2:11-12).

The law of love

At the end of this list of the Spirit's fruit, Paul says to the Galatians, "Against such things there is no law" (5:23). St. Augustine said something similar in another way: "Love God, and do as you please"—the first two words giving restraint to the rest. When the fruit of the Spirit is evident in our lives, it means that our desires have been refocused and we want to be like Jesus. If this is so, laws are not needed because we will want to please Jesus and do what he asks of us. Love will be our law.

Laws are designed to stop people from hurting each other, but when love is in control, laws are not necessary. Living freely under the guidance of love is God's way of life for us, but it is foreign to our natural understanding and desires. When there is a willingness to live in joyful obedience to Jesus, no law is needed.

Earlier in his letter to the Galatians, Paul had challenged the community, asking, "Are you so foolish? After beginning by means of the Spirit, are you now trying to finish by means of the flesh? . . . So again I ask, does God give you his Spirit and work miracles among you by the works of the law, or by your believing what you heard?" (3:3, 5). There is this battle within us between freedom and law. We easily give up our freedom for the security of knowing what is expected of us, what is going to happen next, and how we are to act. But this allows the Holy Spirit very little room in which to work. The traditions and rules by which we live bring us security; the idea that we could let go of some of these and allow the Spirit to guide us is too frightening to contemplate. But the only way the fruit will grow is if we allow the Holy Spirit the freedom to work in us.

There must be a passion for freedom in our hearts. We must be determined to follow the voice of the Holy Spirit even when it means breaking established habits. There is a narrow way between liberty in love and security of habit, and the temptation to give up the struggle is always strong. We must resist it.

3. So how is the fruit produced in our lives?

We need to provide the right conditions if the life of Christ is to flourish and if the fruit is to grow in us. Ripe fruit hanging from the branches of a tree clearly shows that it's a good tree and has been well cared for.

When people hear someone talking about being open to the Holy Spirit and see obvious changes in that person's life, they'll listen because they can see the fruit. But if a tree is to produce good fruit, it must be cultivated, pruned, nurtured, and protected against disease and attacks by pests so that the fruit can ripen and be harvested at the right time. We, too, will produce better fruit if we allow ourselves to be cultivated, pruned, nurtured, and protected. This is how the gifts of the Spirit play an important part: they are tools to produce better fruit in the lives of all of us by addressing those areas in which we need to change and to grow.

A fruit tree needs the right conditions to flourish: water, sunshine, fertilizer, and good soil. We need these things too:

- the water of the Spirit;
- the sunshine of God's love;
- the fertilizer of prayer;
- the good soil of the word of God and the sacraments.

God wants every Christian, who starts life as a seedling, to be fed and protected, blossom in the fullness of time, and bear good fruit. The primary purpose of every plant, bush, or tree is to bear fruit; this is the way it reproduces itself. People looking at Christians should be able to see the fruit and recognize the work of God in us. The fruit of the Spirit will attract them and cause them to want to be like us. But good fruit takes time to grow, and we must be patient. Here is how we can cooperate with God's work in us:

First, in the seed, the life of the plant. The farmer does not create the life; it's already present in the seed, but he must ensure the best conditions for that seed to germinate and grow into a new plant.

The field will need to be prepared: to be weeded, dug over, and fertilized. Our lives may be like a field overgrown with weeds and used as a dumping ground for all sorts of rubbish. We need to acknowledge this and decide to clean it up. There will be some things we can do ourselves, but above all, we need to ask Jesus to work with us through his Holy Spirit. When he gets access to the field—by our invitation—he can start to push things around, to clear away the rubbish that clutters our lives, to help us reorder our priorities, to work with us to pull out the weeds of sin, and to break up the ground of our hardheartedness.

But he won't do anything without us; he needs our cooperation. The fruit is a result of the work of the Spirit within us, and we will need to acknowledge that there are problems in some areas of our lives and hand them over to God. Then we must be obedient as he starts working with us.

Second, in the pruning. Every gardener knows that in order to produce good fruit, a bush or tree must be pruned; excess and unnecessary growth has to be removed. Jesus tells us,

> "I am the true vine, and my Father is the gardener. He cuts off every branch in me that bears no fruit, while every branch that does bear fruit he prunes so that it will be even more fruitful. You are already clean because of the word I have spoken to you. Remain in me, as I also remain in you. No branch can bear fruit by itself; it must remain in the vine. Neither can you bear fruit unless you remain in me." (John 15:1-4)

The message is clear. We are to remain in Christ and accept that some things will have to be pruned—relationships, activities, even ministries and services—so that our lives can be more fruitful.

Finally, in the fruit. Fruit grows—it is not made by us. We do not provide the dynamic, vital force by which God's fruit grows any more than we provide the original seed. It is all from God, but it does require our cooperation. Because the Spirit is alive within us, we will bear fruit, but it will only grow as we surrender more and more to the divine Gardener. It's his garden, and the fruit is for him.

When we desire to live a fuller life in the Holy Spirit, we want the fruit in our lives to increase, and this will happen as long as we are open and do not put up barriers. Much of our slow growth in the things of God is due to the fact that we have some clearing up and sorting out to do, and we are not prepared to receive nearly as much help as we need and that God wants to give us. Sometimes our desires are conditional rather than absolute, and this restricts what the Holy Spirit is able to do in us. If there is little sign of the Holy Spirit's fruit in our lives, it may sometimes be that we are in a dormant period during which God is strengthening our roots, but it is often because we are not cooperating as we should.

Paul tells us that "if the root is holy, so are the branches" (Romans 11:16). He also says, "Just as you received Christ Jesus as Lord, continue to live your lives in him, rooted and built up in him, strengthened in the faith as you were taught, and overflowing with thankfulness" (Colossians 2:6-7). We need to be well rooted in Christ if we're going to bear good fruit.

4. Why are we expected to bear fruit?

If the fruit of the Spirit is growing in us and is clearly visible to others, this will help us to fulfill the words of Jesus when he speaks about another kind of fruit (John 15:8-11). Here he is talking about our fruitfulness in bringing others into relationship with him. In this context, our fruitfulness is seen when our witness to our faith produces new disciples of Jesus so that

- God may be glorified: "This is to my Father's glory, that you bear much fruit" (15:8);
- we may show we are disciples of Jesus, his Son: "Showing yourselves to be my disciples" (15:8);
- the joy of the Lord may be in us: "So that my joy may be in you and that your joy may be complete" (15:11).

The testimony we give, the position we hold in our church, the denomination to which we belong—these say nothing about our spiritual life. The only real evidence of our life in Christ is the fruit that the Holy Spirit causes to grow in us. The one desire common to every form of life is to reproduce itself, to be fruitful. This is true for Christians: each person who has come into new life in Christ is called to reproduce this divine life.

The fruit of the Spirit is Christ's personality expressed through us. When we allow this to grow in every part of our lives, it is Jesus, the first fruit, who will be evident. It has nothing to do with our own effort; it's not Christian character manufactured by some kind of human ability. It's not according to me; it's according to Jesus. When we look at the fruit of the Spirit, we are looking at something we want God to achieve in us with our cooperation.

We must allow the Holy Spirit to form the life of Jesus in us so that the world can see him in us and through us. This will happen as the fruit of the Spirit grows in us.

Come, Holy Spirit!

Questions for Reflection and Discussion

1. The fruit of the Holy Spirit is the nature of Jesus himself becoming more and more evident in our lives. How can we best encourage the growth of the fruit?

2. The Spirit is really one fruit with nine flavors, reflecting the personality of Jesus. How much do I show evidence of the nature of Jesus on a day-to-day basis?

3. Fruit is not given; it grows in us. How can we best deal with the obstacles and hindrances that interfere with this growth?

4. Which of the flavors of the fruit of the Spirit is struggling to grow in your life? Why is this?

Helpful Scripture passagesto pray:
    Galatians 5:13-26
    John 15
    Colossians 2:6-7
    Matthew 7:18

CHAPTER SEVEN

The New Life: Walking in the Spirit

1. What do we mean by "walking in the Spirit," and how do we do it?
2. What are the dangers we must guard against?
3. How do we stay with the Spirit and not slip back into our old ways?

1. What do we mean by "walking in the Spirit," and how do we do it?

In earlier chapters, we saw that the Holy Spirit is a person, promised by the Father and released to us after Jesus had ascended into heaven. He is the presence, the love, the power, and the life of God, given to us here and now to renew us in our relationships to God, to ourselves, and to others. The Spirit is available in his fullness to every Christian, and when he is poured out to work in us, he reveals Jesus as Lord and Savior and God as a loving Father. The Spirit brings love, power, authority, and commitment into our lives. This means that every area of our life can be renewed and revitalized. This is what the prophet Ezekiel prophesied:

> I will give you a new heart and put a new spirit in you; I will remove from you your heart of stone and give you a heart of flesh. And I will put my Spirit in you and move you to follow my decrees and be careful to keep my laws. (36:26-27)

As the prophet Zechariah reminded us, this happens "not by might, nor by power, but by my Spirit, says the Lord Almighty" (4:6).

So, inspired by the Old Testament prophets, when we talk about walking in the Spirit, we mean living this new life, with this new heart, in the love and strength of the Holy Spirit and not by our own might or power. At its most simple, walking in the Spirit means walking with God, in complete unity with him and his purposes, directed and guided by his Holy Spirit. It means putting into practice day after day the new life that Jesus has made available to us. "Since we live by the Spirit, let us keep in step with the Spirit" (Galatians 5:25). Jesus explained it to Nicodemus like this:

> "Very truly I tell you, no one can enter the kingdom of God unless they are born of water and the Spirit. Flesh gives birth to flesh, but the Spirit gives birth to spirit. You should not be surprised at my saying, 'You must be born again.' The wind blows wherever it pleases. You hear its sound, but you cannot tell where it comes from or where it is going. So it is with everyone born of the Spirit." (John 3:5-8)

We are born again when we enter this new life through baptism and the coming of the Holy Spirit, but living it out is not automatic. Even though we know all about it and want to walk in the Spirit and enjoy this new life, the old life is still open to us, and we must be aware of it.

What is the old life? It is a life lived largely by rules. We see Jesus Christ as a man who lived two thousand years ago and we believe that he is God, sent to us by his Father, and we try to follow his teaching and do as he did. We take on his ideals and try to live by them. So we see Christianity as a way of life governed by a set of rules, and we try, by using our willpower, to do what is right and to live as we believe Jesus would want us to live. This approach is very similar to that of the Jewish people at the time of Christ: they tried to live by the law but failed. Even those who wanted to live by the law could not do so, and those whose task it was to teach the law also failed to put it into practice in their own lives or to help others. These teachers came in for harsh condemnation from Jesus: "And you experts in the law, woe to you, because you load people down with burdens they can hardly carry, and you yourselves will not lift one finger to help them" (Luke 11:46).

When we look at the teachings of Jesus—the Sermon on the Mount, for example—we realize that with only the law to help us, we will find it impossible to put his teachings into practice in our lives. Neither a new law nor a new idealism is enough on its own—we need new life.

So what is the new life? It is life in the Holy Spirit, God at work in us. Jesus has supplied us with the power to live a new life through his Holy Spirit—we are his instruments. This means that we rely more on God working in us and through us than on our own efforts to be good and to do the right things. It is a completely new principle of life, not just a few adjustments made to the old way of life.

How do we enter into this new life? We've already seen in chapters 2 and 3 that when we are thirsty, Jesus invites us to come to him and drink (John 7:37). He is the source of the new life.

If we acknowledge our need and want to have new life in the Spirit, then with expectant faith we must ask him to baptize us in his Holy Spirit. God has promised, and he will honor his promise; any barriers to receiving from him will lie with us and not with him. In chapter 3 we looked at what we mean when we speak of being baptized in the Spirit; it is an unconditional surrender to the work of the Spirit in us.

Sometimes life in the Spirit is thought to be anything that is supernatural—that simply because something is supernatural means that it must be in accordance with the Holy Spirit. But we have seen that the Holy Spirit is not the only source of supernatural power, so we need to be careful. If we always equate the supernatural with the Holy Spirit, then it is an easy but dangerous step to define life in the Spirit as life surrounded by supernatural events. Of course, some of what the Holy Spirit does is clearly supernatural—the manifestation of his gifts, for example. But the key to living and walking in the Spirit is being led by the Holy Spirit in both natural and supernatural ways.

To walk in the Spirit is not just to receive direct guidance from God in everything we do. We are also led by the Spirit when we allow God to form us in other ways: through the Scriptures and teaching, through prayer and our commitment to the sacraments and to the life of the Church, and through the Christian community. No one should wait for a direct indication from the Holy Spirit before doing something they know to be right and necessary. Our approach to many things has already been formed by the Lord, and we can remain open to the Spirit without seeking direct guidance for every step on the way. We know God is with us, so we step out in faith and do what we know to be right, trusting he will help us when we need him.

Our goal is always to avoid what is wrong and do what is right and good. However, when we live life in the Spirit, our actions now proceed not just from a code of conduct but from the life of the Spirit in us, which will guide us in natural and supernatural ways:

- We now have the Spirit to guide us, not just the principles of good conduct.
- The presence of God's Spirit will make a difference in what we do.
- The Spirit knows the mind and will of God, and he will reveal it to us.

What will happen as we walk in the Spirit? It may not be dramatic or sudden, but inevitably the life of the Holy Spirit within us will become evident, and things will begin to happen that did not happen before. One clear sign will be the growth of the fruit of the Spirit in us.

But life in the Spirit is not something we achieve as soon as we are baptized in the Holy Spirit. The process of inner transformation is part of walking in the Spirit. Sometimes change will come quickly and easily, but at other times it will be slow and painful. This is all part of "walking the walk." After baptism in the Spirit, there may be a wilderness experience, and we should not be discouraged by this. Jesus himself was taken into the wilderness to be tempted by the devil (Luke 4:1-13).

At times of difficulty and discouragement, we need to

- hold fast to what we believe;
- put our trust in God's promise that "I am with you always" (Matthew. 28:20);
- seek fellowship, prayer, and support from other Christians;
- resist the lies and temptations of the devil.

We will come through our times of trial and be strengthened by them. St. Paul has a very positive view of this: "And we know that in all things God works for the good of those who love him, who have been called according to his purpose" (Romans 8:28). In Galatians he also reminds us,

So I say, walk by the Spirit, and you will not gratify the desires of the flesh. For the flesh desires what is contrary to the Spirit, and the Spirit what is contrary to the flesh. They are in conflict with each other, so that you are not to do whatever you want. But if you are led by the Spirit, you are not under the law. (5:16-18)

Living according to our own self-interest will direct us away from God and towards sin. We cannot live for God and ourselves at the same time—the two things are opposed to each other. So in order to yield to the Holy Spirit, we must resist our sinful nature, sometimes called "the flesh," because as long as we want to maintain ourselves, there will be little room for God. We do not want to "gratify the cravings of our flesh and follow its desires and thoughts" (cf. Ephesians 2:3). The desires of our flesh are against the Spirit, and these desires are of the mind as well as the body. We must die to ourselves so that God can fill us more and more.

2. What are the dangers we must guard against?

The first dangerous temptation we face is pride. Everything we do is for God's glory, not for our glory. It can be hard to accept this and to give God the credit, particularly when we have natural ability and are tempted to bask in the glory of things we have achieved through our own strength. But this is simply a question of pride, and as the proverb reminds us, "Pride goes before destruction, / a haughty spirit before a fall" (Proverbs 16:18).

Baptism in the Holy Spirit is not a sign of superiority; if anything, it underscores our weakness. It is because we are weak that we seek God's strength. When God blesses us, we do not ourselves get any stronger; it is simply that God's strength is now able to flow more freely through us. But the danger of human pride will be lurking in the shadows of our walk in the Spirit. God makes men and women strong in the power of his Spirit and they prosper. The danger is that instead of constantly acknowledging their natural weakness and humbling themselves before God, they can become proud, arrogant, and, finally, presumptuous in his presence. They think themselves without error, above correction—then comes the fall, and exclusion from God's blessing. Paul is an outstanding example of a man who knew his own weaknesses and relied on God's strength: "For when I am weak, then I am strong" (2 Corinthians 12:10). He thanked God for his weakness, and look at what he achieved!

When we are baptized in the Holy Spirit, we are just beginning. As we walk in the Spirit, we will make many mistakes; we will have failures as well as successes. We must never let the successes make us proud; we must not talk too much about them, and we must give all the glory to God. Similarly, we should never allow our failures to lead us into despair. These, too, are stepping stones along the way, not stumbling blocks, and if we are humble, we will learn from our mistakes. The proud never admit mistakes, and so can never learn from them. If we are to be of any use to God, we must admit our failures, learn from others, and accept their correction. Above all, we need to remember the words of Jesus: "Apart from me you can do nothing" (John 15:5).

The second great temptation we face is ourselves. If our ego is not dealt with, our service will be spoiled. Our natural reason and emotions can easily get mixed up with the impulses of the Spirit, especially when we have some knowledge of the matter concerned or are personally involved. It is only humility that will safeguard us from speaking words as inspirations of the Spirit when the source is really our own reason and emotions.

Baptism in the Holy Spirit is no shortcut to Christian maturity; indeed, it often signals the breaking out of fresh conflicts that show us what we are really like. If the Holy Spirit is to be in full control, these conflicts must be resolved, the self must be set aside, and all the glory must go to God. When the Spirit is in full control, we will want to keep out of the limelight and give the glory to God. Sadly, however, it's easy to remain self-centered out of personal glory; we look for experiences rather than service and for personal enjoyment more than self-denial. All this is possible, but only for a limited time;

the power will soon be withdrawn and only human strength will remain. The language may still be used, but the reality will no longer be there.

We must be honest and admit we have failed and allow the Holy Spirit to search us and untangle us. The answer is in humble repentance before God and before others, if necessary. When we slip back into our old ways, it does not mean that the Holy Spirit has left us and that our new life is over. It simply means that there is still more work to be done in us. The fact that the Holy Spirit has started the work in us is the guarantee of its completion (Ephesians 1:14), because when the Spirit comes,

- he inspires prayer; this will maintain our spiritual power (Romans 8:26);
- he brings freedom in praise and worship; this maintains our relationship with God (Acts 16:25);
- he gives some a desire for intercession; this supports others (1 Timothy 2:1);
- he brings power to witness and evangelize; this draws others to Christ (Acts 1:8);
- he brings power for healing and deliverance; this produces wholeness and freedom (Luke 9:1-2);
- he nourishes social concern; this helps us not to become self-centered (Acts 2:44-45);
- he gives access to his gifts and ministries; this builds up the body of Christ (1 Corinthians 12:4-31);
- but most of all, he brings a new freedom (Galatians 5:1).

In the Pentecost meeting with the new movements and
ecclesial communities in St. Peter's Square on May 30, 1998,
to which I referred earlier and at which I was present, Pope
St. John Paul II said this:

> Today, I would like to cry out to all of you gathered here in St
> Peter's Square and to all Christians: Open yourselves docilely
> to the gifts of the Spirit! Accept gratefully and obediently the
> charisms which the Spirit never ceases to bestow on us! Do
> not forget that every charism is given for the common good,
> that is, for the benefit of the whole Church. . . . Today, from
> this upper room in St. Peter's Square, a great prayer rises:
> Come, Holy Spirit, come and renew the face of the earth!
> Come with your seven gifts! Come, Spirit of life, Spirit of
> communion and love! The Church and the world need you.
> Come, Holy Spirit, and make ever more fruitful the charisms
> you have bestowed on us. Give new strength and missionary
> zeal to these sons and daughters of yours who have gathered
> here. Open their hearts; renew their Christian commitment in
> the world. Make them courageous messengers of the gospel,
> witnesses to the risen Jesus Christ, the Redeemer and Savior of
> man. Strengthen their love and their fidelity to the Church.[32]

There must be a passion for freedom in our hearts and an
openness to receive from the Holy Spirit. If we are to be courageous messengers of the gospel and witnesses of Jesus, we must
be determined to hear the voice of the Spirit and to follow him,
even when it means breaking established patterns and habits.
The Church needs all of us to use our gifts to play a fully active
part in her life and mission. As Pope John Paul II explained,

The Spirit is like a wind filling the sails of the great ship of the Church. If, however, we look at her closely, she uses numerous other small sails that are the hearts of the baptized. Everyone, dear friends, is invited to hoist his sail and unfurl it with courage, to permit the Spirit to act with all his sanctifying power. By allowing the Spirit to act in one's own life, one also makes the best contribution to the Church's mission. *Do not be afraid . . . to unfurl your sails to the breath of the Spirit!*[33]

In our first chapter, we looked at some of the words used to describe the Holy Spirit. As we come to the end of our journey in *An Invitation to the Spirit-Filled Life*, let's look again at some of those words and remind ourselves of the richness of their meanings when used to describe the Spirit of God.

- *Wind:* dramatic and powerful, gentle and caressing.

- *Fire:* consuming and destroying, but energy and heat producing.

- *Cloud:* moving or static, overshadowing, concealing, holding the promise of rain.

- *Water:* cleansing, life-giving, refreshing.

- *Oil:* heat and light-producing, healing, a sign of consecration, a link to the sacraments.

- *Breath:* essential for life, creative.

- *Light:* a sign of the presence of God, helping us "see" spiritually.

- *Dove:* symbol of peace and love, freedom and flight.

We need to become familiar with every attribute of the Holy Spirit: his power, his love, his creativity, his energy, and, above all, his freedom. He will light a fire of love within us that will burn away our inhibitions and enable us to be salt and light for our world. We will commit ourselves to a new obedience and discover a new desire to serve with power. It is not enough to know him—we must let ourselves be empowered and led by the Spirit.

This brings us to our final question.

3. How do we stay with the Spirit and not slip back into our old ways?

It's quite possible to fall out of the principle of grace and to bring ourselves under the law again. We saw earlier how angry Paul was when he saw the Galatian Christians allowing this to happen. He spoke quite directly to them:

You foolish Galatians! Who has bewitched you? Before your very eyes Jesus Christ was clearly portrayed as crucified. I would like to learn just one thing from you: Did you receive the Spirit by the works of the law, or by believing what you heard? Are you so foolish? After beginning by means of the Spirit, are you now trying to finish by means of the flesh? Have you experienced so much in vain—if it really was in vain? So again I ask, does God give you his Spirit and work miracles among you by the works of the law, or by your believing what you heard? (3:1-5)

The Galatians wanted to have Christ but also to keep the Old Testament law. Having started in the Spirit, they were trying to reach the finish line by their own natural energy and strength. In chapter 7 of Romans, Paul tells us that when he starts thinking about the law and trying to keep it, he is distracted from Christ and his provision of new life in the Holy Spirit and so falls back into the old impotence and frustration. Only when he concentrates again on Christ and takes himself back into walking in the Spirit is he able to serve again with power: "By dying to what once bound us, we have been released from the law so that we serve in the new way of the Spirit, and not in the old way of the written code" (Romans 7:6).

Some who start their new lives in the Spirit rejoicing in the free provision of God's grace go on to try to reform themselves and society by their own natural energy and run into frustration and failure. To be baptized in the Holy Spirit is to realize afresh that, in everything, we are to live, not out of ourselves and our own efforts, but out of God's provision of life and power in Christ. Jesus said we are called to be salt and light:

"You are the salt of the earth. But if the salt loses its saltiness, how can it be made salty again? It is no longer good for anything, except to be thrown out and trampled underfoot. You are the light of the world. A town built on a hill cannot be hidden. Neither do people light a lamp and put it under a bowl. Instead they put it on its stand, and it gives light to everyone in the house. In the same way, let your light shine before others, that they may see your good deeds and glorify your Father in heaven." (Matthew 5:13-16)

If we are to remain "salty" and light-giving, we need the power of the Spirit filling our lives. To be filled with the Holy Spirit is to turn

- from law to Spirit;
- from works to faith;
- from self to God.

To walk in the Spirit is to

- walk in the love, the freedom, and the power of God;
- listen to the voice and guidance of the Holy Spirit;
- do everything in the Spirit's strength, not our own;
- do it all for the glory of Jesus and our Father.

When we walk in the will of God, we will have peace and will know when we divert from his path. Christ died to give us freedom; let's accept it now and walk with him in the power and freedom of his Spirit. Then we'll begin to experience the Spirit-filled life!

Come, Holy Spirit!

Questions for Reflection and Discussion

1. Through the work of Jesus, it is now possible for us to live a new life in the Spirit, but it isn't automatic. Why not?

2. As we walk in this new life in the Spirit, there are many dangers, especially pride and self-interest, that will hinder us. What else may restrict us?

3. As we live our Christian lives, it's important to stay with the Spirit and avoid the temptation to return to our old ways. What can we do to avoid the risk of slipping back?

4. Explain in your own words what it means to "walk in the Spirit" day by day.

Helpful Scripture passages to pray:
    Ezekiel 36:26-27
    Romans 7:6
    Galatians 3:1
    Matthew 5:13-16

Epilogue:
The Century of the Holy Spirit

The twentieth century is often referred to as the "century of the Holy Spirit." From the beginning, it was characterized by a series of amazing outpourings of the Spirit, which occurred in different places from 1900 onward. As the century began, on January 1, 1901, Pope Leo XIII prayed that the Holy Spirit would come again in power to the whole Church, and he sang the *Veni Creator Spiritus* ("Come, Creator Spirit") in his private chapel. Perhaps to his surprise, the first sign of an answer to his prayer was an experience of the presence and power of the Holy Spirit at that moment at the Bethel Bible School in Topeka, Kansas. This was followed in 1906 by a revival in a poor, run-down mission church pastored by William J. Seymour at 312 Azusa Street in Los Angeles, California. Revival had also broken out in Wales in 1904–5 under Evan Roberts, a twenty-six-year-old lay minister in the Free Church chapels of the coal-mining valleys. These events heralded the arrival of the Pentecostal and charismatic movements, which within a few years would be found all over the world.

As the century unfolded, a variety of traditional Protestant churches—Anglican, Episcopalian, Lutheran, Reformed, Methodist, and Baptist—also experienced renewal in the power of the Spirit, and from the 1950s onward, the independent New Church or House Church movement appeared in the United Kingdom and North America, quickly becoming established and spreading rapidly. Typical of these would be Pioneer, New

Frontiers, and, later, the Vineyard churches. Only the Catholic and Orthodox Churches seemed unaffected by this new outpouring of the Spirit. Then in 1967, a group of American Catholic students from Duquesne University in Pittsburgh were attending a weekend retreat at which they, too, experienced an amazing outpouring of the Holy Spirit as they studied the early chapters of the Book of Acts. Signs of the Holy Spirit at work followed in some Orthodox churches, and to complete the picture, Messianic Judaism was born. The common factor shared by the Pentecostals, the charismatics in the mainline denominations, the New or House Churches, and some other charismatic nondenominational churches was baptism in the Holy Spirit and the reemergence of the *charismata*, the gifts of the Holy Spirit.

These special outpourings of the Holy Spirit had a number of things in common:

- All were grassroots events.
- All were characterized by great love, joy, and missionary zeal.
- All experienced artistic creativity, new music, songwriting, and worship.
- There was a greater awareness and interest in the Second Coming of Christ.
- The charisms, the supernatural gifts of the Holy Spirit, were freely poured out.
- There was a new appreciation of a shared experience, leading to a growing ecumenism.
- Most had to face negativity, criticism, and even rejection by other churches, and, in the case of some of the

denominational churches, negativity from their hierarchies and many members.

- Their experience was everywhere described as baptism in the Holy Spirit.

So what effect did all of this have on the worldwide church in all its different expressions, and what changes in attitudes and practices resulted? Not surprising, these shared experiences gave rise to a much greater openness to Christians from other denominations, churches, and fellowships. In the early days, especially, the grace and power of the Spirit were often mediated to us through Christians outside our own circles, and this made us more aware of how much we had in common and how much we needed each other. God seemed less concerned about our divisions than we were, and we read with new eyes the words of Jesus in which he prayed for unity for all his followers (John 17:20-23). We really understood from Ephesians 4:3 that there *is* a fundamental unity we are all called to keep. We *are* brothers and sisters in Christ because we all declare him our Savior and Lord and share in a common baptism.

Pope St. John Paul II noted, "At the Second Vatican Council, the Catholic Church committed herself *irrevocably* to following the path of the ecumenical venture."[34] Popes Blessed Paul VI, St. John Paul II, Benedict XVI, and Francis have all emphasized the important contribution to be made by those who have experienced a new outpouring of the Spirit in their lives. We have a special calling to establish closer relationships and friendships with those from other Christian expressions and traditions, but if we are to do this effectively, we must first be sure of our own identity. In order for true and valid ecumenism to exist, those involved must be faithful to who they are and must accept others as they are. It cannot be a matter of the lowest common denominator—that is not authentic ecumenism.

In Pope St. John Paul II's encyclical letter *Ut Unum Sint* (That They May Be One), published in 1995, he again encouraged all Catholics to see other Christians as brothers and sisters in Christ, to meet and pray with them, to dialogue and share with them, to learn about them and from them, to do together whatever can be done in good conscience, and to give public witness to our shared faith alongside them. He fully acknowledged that this would not be easy and that many Catholics would be challenged by it. But he asked us to look deeply into our hearts and acknowledge our weaknesses and past failings before the Lord, fully recognizing that while we must all play our parts, full unity is something only the Holy Spirit can bring about. We must work for it, pray for it, and allow the Spirit to make it happen. We are, after all, those who know the power of the Spirit.

The powerful outpourings of the Holy Spirit, experienced by so many different parts of the body of Christ in the twentieth century in particular, have shown us just how much the worldwide Christian family needs the love, grace, and power of the Spirit of God to bring us new life and equip us for all that lies ahead. The Spirit helps us grow in love for God, for ourselves, and for one another, and he gives us both the desire and the power to evangelize. To do that effectively, there needs to be a basic unity among us, "so that the world may believe that you have sent me" (John 17:21).

Let's now look briefly at the Catholic Charismatic Renewal, a very important part of this mighty move of God's Holy Spirit.

The Catholic Charismatic Renewal

Many people have heard something about the Catholic Charismatic Renewal (CCR) and, without really understanding what it is, may well have decided that it's not for them. That's a great pity. It's a gift from God and has something very important to contribute to the life of the Church, as we have already seen. So against this background, I will try to summarize, in a short and easy-to-understand way, what lies at the heart of the Catholic Charismatic Renewal and why it is important to the Church. I'll begin by looking at the two key words "charismatic" and "renewal" as used in this context.

A charism is a special gift of the Holy Spirit. Its root is in the Greek word *charis*, meaning "grace." Every charism is a special gift of grace because it is supernaturally given by the Holy Spirit to equip the recipient to undertake particular tasks or services for the benefit of the Church. So the word "charismatic" is used here to describe something that has its origins in, is inspired by, and contains the power of the Holy Spirit.

The Oxford English Dictionary defines "renewal" in these words: "among charismatic Christians, the state or process of being renewed in the Holy Spirit." So renewal is a process, usually beginning when the Holy Spirit responds to someone's request to renew his spiritual life. Every Christian needs ongoing spiritual renewal, and here we are clearly reminded that this is an activity of the Holy Spirit. In fact, Pope Francis has explained the Charismatic Renewal in these words: "You, the Charismatic Renewal, have received a great gift from the

Lord. Your movement's birth was willed by the Holy Spirit to be 'a current of grace in the Church and for the Church.' This is your identity: to be a current of grace."[35]

Drawing all this together, we can say that the Catholic Charismatic Renewal is in essence both the action and the result of an outpouring of the Holy Spirit, which brings a new or renewed experience of God's life and power into the lives of his people. It is a sovereign work of the Holy Spirit of God because it is not something we own or control. Through it we are invited to hand our lives over to God and to give the control back to him. We allow God to be God and to work in us through his Holy Spirit to equip and empower us to live effective Christian lives. This renewal is freely offered to anyone who asks—we just need to be willing to invite the Holy Spirit to release his power in us and bring alive the graces of our baptism. But the Spirit not only brings alive all that we have already received through the sacraments of our Christian initiation. He also comes again in power to equip us with new gifts for service and mission.

The Beginnings

A key part of Pope St. John XXIII's motivation in calling the Second Vatican Council in the early 1960s was a desire to see the Holy Spirit bring new vision and power into the life of the worldwide Church. So he invited every Catholic to join him in praying for an opening of the windows of the Church to the wind of the Spirit, for a new Pentecost in our time. God answered the prayers of his people, and among the many fruits of the council were a much greater appreciation of the gifts of the Holy Spirit in the life of the Church and a blossoming of new ecclesial movements and communities.

Among these we find the Catholic Charismatic Renewal (CCR), which began in February 1967 among a group of about twenty-five American students from Duquesne University who attended a weekend retreat at which they experienced an amazing outpouring of the Holy Spirit. Two of their leaders had already seen their own spiritual lives transformed through the power of the Holy Spirit at a Protestant prayer meeting when hands were laid on them, and this had stirred in them a new spiritual hunger and thirst. As they and the students read from the first four chapters of the Book of Acts, the question they were asking was why did their own experience of God lack the power and effects they were reading about among the first disciples of Jesus? As they prayed in the chapel at the retreat house for a renewal of their confirmation grace, they experienced a sovereign move of the Holy Spirit as God revealed to them his majesty, his glory, and his merciful love in a powerful "upper room" experience. This was the experience we usually call baptism in the Holy Spirit.

From these simple beginnings, baptism in the Holy Spirit spread rapidly through the campuses of the Catholic universities in the United States and into the wider Church. No grassroots spiritual movement has ever spread as far or as fast as the CCR, and ten years later, more than one hundred million Catholics in over one hundred countries could testify to similar experiences. Today there are charismatic Catholics in more than two hundred countries.

In his 1991 letter to Patti Gallagher Mansfield, one of the Duquesne weekend retreatants, Pentecostal church historian

Dr. Vinson Synan wrote, "One never knows the effect of any one meeting when the Spirit of God moves. I believe the 'Duquesne Weekend' will have to go down in history as one of the most important prayer meetings that ever occurred, especially in modern times."[36]

The Church Hierarchy

From the very beginning, following a time of careful discernment and theological and pastoral reflection, the Church has welcomed the Catholic Charismatic Renewal. Blessed Pope Paul VI received the early leaders in Rome in 1973 and again in 1975, when he described the CCR as "a chance for the Church and the world."[37] On numerous public occasions, Pope John Paul II expressed his personal support. For example, he said, "Because of the Spirit, the church preserves a continual youthful vitality. And the Charismatic Renewal is an eloquent manifestation of this vitality today, a bold statement of 'what the Spirit is saying to the Churches' (Revelation 2:7)!" Similarly, Pope Emeritus Benedict XVI has been unfailing in his commitment and encouragement before, during, and after his term as supreme pontiff, and Pope Francis prayed, sang with, and spoke to fifty thousand charismatic Catholics in Olympic Stadium in Rome in 2014.

In 1993, during my first term as president, the International Council of the Catholic Charismatic Renewal was given official recognition and granted formal Church statutes as a body to promote the CCR throughout the Church. So the Catholic Charismatic Renewal is not some strange fringe organization. It is an accepted, approved, and encouraged current of fruitful life at the very heart of the Catholic Church, bringing new life and spiritual power to millions of ordinary men and women.

What Form Does the Catholic Charismatic Renewal Take?

The CCR is not a single, unified worldwide movement, and it does not have a human founder or formal program of initiation and membership list as other movements do. Neither is it a special devotion to the Holy Spirit, a new spirituality for some particular people, or just a network of prayer groups and communities. In 1990, Cardinal Leon Josef Suenens explained it in these words:

> To interpret the Renewal as a movement among other movements is to misunderstand its nature: it is a movement of the Spirit offered to the entire Church, and destined to rejuvenate every facet of the Church's life. The soul of Renewal, Baptism in the Spirit, is a grace of Pentecostal refreshment offered to all Christians.[38]

The CCR is a highly diverse collection of individuals, groups, communities, ministries, and activities, usually quite independent of one another, in different stages and modes of development and with different emphases. One of the special characteristics of the CCR is the enormous variety of its expressions and ministries, all inspired by the Holy Spirit and carried out in his power, which have a home under the CCR umbrella. Everyone shares the same foundational experience of the empowering presence of the Holy Spirit through baptism in the Spirit, but the emphasis is on relationships and networks rather than on structures and organization. Pope Francis exhorted a gathering of Catholic charismatics,

> You, the people of God, the people of the charismatic renewal, must be careful not to lose the freedom which the Holy Spirit has given you! The danger for the renewal . . . is that of getting too organized: the danger of excessive planning. . . . Another danger is that of becoming *arbiters* of God's grace . . . , managers of grace. . . . You are *dispensers* of God's grace, not its *arbiters*![39]

These patterns of informal relationships are to be found at local, diocesan, national, and international levels and are characterized by free association, dialogue, and collaboration. Many groups feel they are part of a big charismatic family which, by their very nature, are related to each other. So they do not see any need to be formally integrated into an ordered charismatic structure locally or nationally. They know they are already fully part of the Church under the hierarchy, and that's what is important to them.

The CCR does not exist to build up a large organization. The simple desire of those involved is that as many others as possible should also have their Christian lives renewed by the Holy Spirit. Some organization may be necessary to facilitate this, but it should be kept to a minimum. In a General Audience on October 12, 1966, Blessed Pope Paul VI reminded us, "If we really love the Church, the main thing we must do is to foster in it an outpouring of the Divine Paraclete, the Holy Spirit."[40]

So with these points in mind, the following simple structures exist within the Charismatic Renewal:

- Diocesan Service Committees (DSCs) that relate to the local bishop and serve the CCR groups in the diocese.
- National Service Committees (NSCs) that perform the same function at the national level and relate to their national conferences of bishops.
- International Catholic Charismatic Renewal Services (ICCRS), which has its office in Vatican premises in Rome. It relates to the Church primarily through the Pontifical Council for Laity, communicating and serving the worldwide CCR and building relationships with the other ecclesial movements in the Church, while maintaining a particular openness to other expressions and parts of the body of Christ outside the Catholic Church.
- The Catholic Fraternity of Covenant Communities, serving the large number of new charismatic communities worldwide that have sprung up as another fruit of the CCR.
- Under Pope Francis, ICCRS and the Catholic Fraternity are working very closely together and sharing a Vatican office.

In their 1991 book *Fanning the Flame*, Killian McDonnell and George Montague explain why the Catholic Charismatic Renewal has not attempted to build up a large organization and structure but simply wants to release the grace of baptism in the Spirit in the lives of all Christians. I believe this is important to remember:

Baptism in the Spirit is captive to no camp, whether liberal or conservative. Nor is it identified with any one movement, nor with one style of prayer, worship, or community. On the contrary, we believe that the gift of Baptism in the Holy Spirit belongs to the Christian inheritance of all those sacramentally initiated into the Church.[41]

Although the CCR differs from other new movements as outlined above, it is generally spoken of by the Church as a movement and, therefore, very much included in the statements about the movements made over recent years by all of the various popes and a number of bishops' conferences. For example, in his document on the state of the Catholic Church in Europe, *Ecclesia in Europa*, we find the following comments by Pope John Paul II:

The Gospel continues to bear fruit in . . . lay associations, in groups devoted to prayer and the apostolate, . . . as well as through the presence and growth of new movements and ecclesial realities. In each of them, the one Spirit finds ways of awakening renewed dedication to the Gospel, generous openness to the service of others, and a Christian life marked by Gospel radicalism and missionary zeal.[42]

These words are certainly true of the Catholic Charismatic Renewal, a current of grace in the great river of the Church, bringing the power of Pentecost into every part of her life and mission and offering a fuller life in the Spirit to everyone.

Charles Whitehead

Endnotes

1. Karl Rahner, *The Trinity* (London: Burns and Oats), 1970, p. 11.
2. *On the Trinity*, 15. Pope Benedict XVI outlined these three insights of St. Augustine on the Holy Spirit in an address at World Youth Day in Sydney, Australia in July 19, 2008, which can be accessed at http://w2.vatican.va/content/benedict-xvi/en/speeches/2008/july/documents/hf_ben-xvi_spe_20080719_vigil.html.
3. Paul VI, *Evangelii Nuntiandi,* 41.
4. *Power for Living,* sponsored and published in 1985 by the Arthur S. DeMoss Foundation.
5. Paul VI, General Audience, November 29, 1972. Available in Italian at http://w2.vatican.va/content/paul-vi/it/audiences/1972/documents/hf_p-vi_aud_19721129.html.
6. John Paul II, *Ecclesia in Europa,* 49.
7. St. Augustine, *Tractates on the Gospel of John,* 74.2.
8. Francis, Address to the Participants in the 37th National Convocation of the Renewal in the Holy Spirit, Olympic Stadium, June 1, 2014. Accessed at http://w2.vatican.va/content/francesco/en/speeches/2014/june/documents/papa-francesco_20140601_rinnovamento-spirito-santo.html.
9. Benedict XVI, Address to Participants in a Course Organized by the Congregation for Evangelization of Peoples. Accessed at http://w2.vatican.va/content/benedict-xvi/en/speeches/2010/september/documents/hf_ben-xvi_spe_20100911_seminario-evang.html.
10. Thomas Aquinas, *Summa Theologica I*, "The Mission of the Divine Persons," Article 6.
11. Paul VI, *Evangelii Nuntiandi,* 75.
12. David Barrett, *World Christian Encyclopedia*, Oxford, 2001.
13. Benedict XVI, General Audience, October 21, 2009. Accessed at http://w2.vatican.va/content/benedict-xvi/en/audiences/2009/documents/hf_ben-xvi_aud_20091021.html.
14. John Paul II, *Ecclesia in Europa,* 65.
15. Ibid., 74.

16. Francis, Address to the Participants in the 37th National Convocation of the Renewal in the Holy Spirit, Olympic Stadium, June 1, 2014.

17. Self-published pamphlet, Rev. Stanley Jebb, April 1973, entitled *The Baptism in the Holy Spirit.*

18. Benedict XVI, Regina Caeli, St. Peter's Square, May 11, 2008. Accessed at http://w2.vatican.va/content/benedict-xvi/en/angelus/2008/documents/hf_ben-xvi_reg_20080511_pentecoste.html.

19. Benedict XVI, Homily, Feast of the Baptism of the Lord, January 13, 2008. Accessed at http://w2.vatican.va/content/benedict-xvi/en/homilies/2008/documents/hf_ben-xvi_hom_20080113_battesimo.html.

20. Vatican II, *Lumen Gentium*, 12.

21. John Paul II, Meeting with Ecclesial Movements and New Communities, May 30, 1998. Accessed at http://w2.vatican.va/content/john-paul-ii/en/speeches/1998/may/documents/hf_jp-ii_spe_19980530_riflessioni.html.

22. Paul VI, General Audience, November 15, 1972. Available in Italian at http://w2.vatican.va/content/paul-vi/it/audiences/1972/documents/hf_p-vi_aud_19721115.html

23. Congregation for the Doctrine of the Faith, *Instruction on Prayers for Healing,* 2.

24. Anglican Bishop Morris Maddocks lived from 1928 to 2008 and was very important in the healing ministry in the UK. He wrote this in an article, and I also heard him say the same thing in a talk on one occasion.

25. Francis, Address to the Participants in the 37th National Convocation of the Renewal in the Holy Spirit, Olympic Stadium, June 1, 2014.

26. *Interior Castle*, Book VI, 10, taken from *The Collected Works of St. Teresa of Avila*, trans. Kieran Kavanaugh, OCD, and Otilio Rodriguez, OCD. Accessed at http://archive.org/stream/SantaTeresaDeAvilaWorksComplete/SaintTeresaOfAvilaCollectedWorksComplete_djvu.txt.

27. St. Augustine, *On the Psalms,* 100.4.

28. St. Gregory the Great, *Moralia,* 8.88.

29. St. Hilary of Poitiers, *Tract on the Psalms*, 64.14-15.

30. St. Cyril of Jerusalem, *Catechetical Lectures*, 17.19.
31. John Paul II, Meeting with Ecclesial Movements and New Communities, May 30, 1998.
32. Ibid.
33. John Paul II, Address to the Superiors and Students of Archdiocesan Seminary of Florence, April 30, 1998. Accessed at http://w2.vatican.va/content/john-paul-ii/en/speeches/1998/april/documents/hf_jp-ii_spe_19980430_arcidiocesi-firenze.html.
34. John Paul II, *Ut Unum Sint*, 3.
35. Francis, Address to Participants in the 37th National Convocation of the Renewal in the Holy Spirit, Olympic Stadium, June 1, 2014.
36. This letter was written in February 1991 and is still in the possession of Patti Gallagher Mansfield.
37. "A chance for the Church and the world" is a quotation from the address of Pope Paul VI to the Catholic Charismatic Renewal leaders on the occasion of the Second International Leaders Conference in Rome on May 19, 1975. The full text is quoted on pages 16 and 17 in *Then Peter Stood Up,* published by International Catholic Charismatic Renewal Services in Vatican City in February 2000.
38. From an article written by Cardinal Leon Josef Suenens called "A Spiritual Journey" for Good News Magazine in 1990, published by the National Service Committee for England.
39. Francis, Address to Participants in the 37th National Convocation of the Renewal in the Holy Spirit, Olympic Stadium, June 1, 2014.
40. Paul VI, General Audience, October 12, 1966. Available in Italian at http://w2.vatican.va/content/paul-vi/it/audiences/1966/documents/hf_p-vi_aud_19661012.html.
41. Killian McDonnell and George T. Montague, *Fanning the Flame*: *What Does Baptism in the Holy Spirit Have to Do with Christian Initiation* (Collegeville, MN: Liturgical Press), 1991.
42. John Paul II, *Ecclesia in Europa*, 15.

the WORD
among us ®
The *Spirit* of Catholic Living

T his book was published by The Word Among Us. Since 1981, The Word Among Us has been answering the call of the Second Vatican Council to help Catholic laypeople encounter Christ in the Scriptures.

The name of our company comes from the prologue to the Gospel of John and reflects the vision and purpose of all of our publications: to be an instrument of the Spirit, whose desire is to manifest Jesus' presence in and to the children of God. In this way, we hope to contribute to the Church's ongoing mission of proclaiming the gospel to the world so that all people would know the love and mercy of our Lord and grow more deeply in their faith as missionary disciples.

Our monthly devotional magazine, *The Word Among Us*, features meditations on the daily and Sunday Mass readings, and currently reaches more than one million Catholics in North America and another half million Catholics in one hundred countries around the world. Our book division, The Word Among Us Press, publishes numerous books, Bible studies, and pamphlets that help Catholics grow in their faith.

To learn more about who we are and what we publish, log on to our website at www.wau.org. There you will find a variety of Catholic resources that will help you grow in your faith.

Embrace His Word, Listen to God . . .

www.wau.org